"Cathy has put together a life-philosophy that will help you think and take action in the direction of your dream. Keep this book within arm's reach, refer to it often, and your life will never be the same!"
-Mark LeBlanc, author of *Growing Your Business*

"If you're ready to start standing up for what you want, need, and deserve, buy this book. It is packed with thought-provoking quotes, real-life anecdotes, and specific suggestions on how to take wise (not rash) risks so you are building the quality of life you want now, not someday. Read it and reap."
- Sam Horn, author of *Tongue Fu!* and *POP! Stand Out in Any Crowd*

"*Living in Full Swing*" will help you find courage you didn't know was in you and use it to your decided advantage."
-Victoria Moran, author of *Creating a Charmed Life*

"When I finished reading this book, I felt like kissing it because of the delightful way Cathy inspires us to take charge of days and make our minutes count."
-- Chuc Barnes, CSP, author of *Get Your Ducks in A Row!* and *Capture the Moment*

"Tired of 'one of those days'? Newton's book *Living in Full Swing* propels you into action. Here's your plan to make someday into today with purposeful risk taking."
-Dorinda Nicholson, Author of *Pearl Harbor Child* *Pearl Harbor Warriors*

"Cathy Newton lays out an exciting framework for calculated risk taking while courageously revealing much of her own life and struggles. As a manager, business owner, husband, parent and friend, this book reminds me of the need to take risks to achieve dynamic results in all aspects of my life."
-Stephen R. Bough, The Law Firm of Stephen R. Bough

"*Living in Full Swing* reminds us that life is an unpredictable adventure. Cathy Newton presents her ideas with a flowing rhythm, as if on a swing ride. As soon as I finished reading it, I wanted to flip it around and start all over again!
-Marina O'Sullivan, International Aviation Program Manager

"Cathy Newton has intertwined well-referenced behavioral science with real-life personal experiences. This book has the substance to inspire people to get back in the swing of purposeful risk taking."
- James R. LaSalle, D.O., Fellow of the American Academy of Family Practice

ALSO BY CATHY NEWTON

RISK IT! Empowering Young People to Become Positive Risk Takers in the Classroom and in Life

It Takes Character

LIVING IN FULL
Swing

Mary Sue & Chuck,

Happy Risking!

Cathy Newton

LIVING IN FULL
Swing

ENJOY THE THRILL OF A NEW LIFE MINDSET,
GET THE MOST OUT OF YOUR RELATIONSHIPS,
GO AHEAD... YOU CAN RISK IT!

CATHY NEWTON

Published by Advantage, Charleston, South Carolina. Member of Advantage Media Group.

ADVANTAGE is a registered trademark and the Advantage colophon is a trademark of Advantage Media Group, Inc.

Printed in the United States of America

ISBN: 978-1-59932-037-3
Library of Congress Control Number: 2007923211

Most Advantage Media Group titles are available at special quantity discounts for bulk purchases for sales promotions, premiums, fundraising, and educational use. Special versions or book excerpts can also be created to fit specific needs.

For more information, please write: Special Markets, Advantage Media Group, P.O. Box 272, Charleston, SC 29402 or call 1.866.775.1696.

This book is dedicated to my family who helped me learn to take the right risks:

my parents Bob and Toni Griggs; my three brothers Dan, Gary, Jamey and my sister Nancy Napoli; my husband Grundy and his two sons Lance and Clint.

TABLE OF CONTENTS

A centuries old axiom about living life to its fullest paraphrased in modern day vernacular might go like this: *"to be successful, a person must have as much regard for the importance of others as they do for themselves"*. This axiom, steeped in religious and philosophical antiquity, is as contemporary as this morning's edition of *USA Today*. Those who are successful in living life to its fullest have learned the power that's contained in these two great dynamics about personal success…how we regard others and how we regard ourselves. Those who have taken this golden rule to the bank have invested in the right risks for the right reasons.

Cathy Newton has been embracing both concepts over the last thirty years that I have known her. As an educator, speaker, trainer and writer, Cathy has demonstrated great insights into how people can get more from their own performance. These insights have made a difference to thousands of participants in her presentations on risk taking around the United States.

Cathy's latest book *Living in Full Swing* will benefit those who want to take their performance up a notch. Cathy understands how you can improve your performance through purposeful risk taking. She makes it understandable through personal examples, anecdotes and practical strategies that can be applied to anyone's experience. This book will help you break out of the safety net in which your mind is imprisoned. It will challenge you to stretch your expectations for yourself and the value you provide in your relationships with others.

I spent a quarter century training and motivating people in my career at Enterprise Rent-A-Car where I retired as the Vice President of Corporate Training. During that career, I met few people who better exemplified *"put your money where your mouth is"* by practicing what they preached more than Cathy.

Reading this book will be the next best thing to having Cathy spend a couple hours chatting with you personally in your living room. She has developed some great concepts that will delight you and inspire you, and when applied, will get you back in the swing of embracing life to its fullest.

- JERRY MCKENNEY
Training Specialist, effectUs, Inc.
(Retired VP Corporate Training, Enterprise Rent-A-Car)

The process of writing a book is a personal quest by the author, yet it is affected by many other people. Family, friends and associates offer insight, ideas, and inspiration. Some are the stimulus for stories and anecdotes. Others offer technical direction and correction. I want to make sure my supportive people know how much I appreciate their assistance. I send many thanks to my mastermind colleagues Candy Whirley, Kathleen Randall, Pam Newman, Chuc Barnes, and Steven Iwersen for stimulating my thinking and cheering my ideas; to Sam Horn for creative coaching; and to writing instructor Ellen Macaulay for wonderful lessons and advice. I send gratitude to special friends Jerry and Barbara McKenney, Tom and Marina O'Sullivan, Jamiel and Linda Yameen, Mike and Elaine Yankunas, Joe and Julie Fallon, Ron and Linda DeJong, Steve and Judith Shoot, Darlene Huff, Karen Griggs, Bernie Martincich, and Jane Ann Gorsky who unconditionally support me and my work. I send appreciation to Charlie Rees at Expressive Images Portrait Studio in Basehor KS for capturing just the right photo of me for the back cover. The staff at Advantage Media Group has been supportive and smart with every step of the publishing process and I send special thanks to Benjamin Toy in sales, Ann Summer for superb editing and positive energy, Amy Ropp for a terrific cover design and Dave Welday for creative guidance. Of course, I send love and thanks to my family for years of encouragement. And I especially thank my husband Grundy for being my anchor in love and in life.

Get in the swing. RISK IT!

*T*here's an old-fashioned porch swing on the screened veranda off the back of my house. We live in the country and the veranda overlooks the Sandbranch Creek, a lovely little strip of woods and a cornfield. I like to take my morning coffee out on the veranda, sit on the swing and enjoy the view. It's a relaxing place to be.

I love to swing. When I was young, I remember needing a little push to get in the groove of swinging. "Higher, Daddy. Push me higher," I would say. But I quickly learned to pump and glide on my own. I still take pleasure from the rhythmic back and forth swaying motion.

Life is full of motion. There are ups and downs, rights and lefts, and curves that turn you every which way but loose. "Strive for balance," some say. For me, the word "balance" doesn't resonate. I think of the scales of justice and the attempt to balance both sides, to make it even and still. That mental image is too static and immobile for me. Life is all about performance and it requires that pump and glide action to make something happen. So, I think that **get in the swing** is a better metaphor.

Another popular notion proclaims: *We are human beings, not human doings.* I'm all for a greater awareness of being present to the good things in life. But I disagree with the slogan. We **are** human doings. We live in a society where people are constantly doing something—for instant gratification, for fulfilling a work ethic, or for somebody else. We are inundated with **do** queries: *What do you **do** for a living? Why did you **do** that? How did you **do** it? What do you think you are **doing**?*

*	**Do** something around here. **Do** that to me one more time. Oh, you think you have a lot to **do**, let me tell you what I have to **do**.*

Are you struggling with a multitude of things to do, with trying to pay attention to the moment, and with the issue of balance? Most people want to perform admirably with a richer sense of personal growth. So, here's the reality: If you want a higher level of achievement, it's in the *swing* and it's in the *doing*. And that's risky business. Striving for success is ultimately about RISK TAKING. No risk, negative risk, or purposeful risk.

> *"If your life is ever going to get better, you'll have to take risks. There is simply no way you can grow without taking chances."*
>
> *-David Viscott*

Risk. It's a little word that commands some big feelings. Are you a risk taker? How you respond to that question depends on how you view that four-letter word RISK? In your mind is it positive or negative? Is it adventurous or hazardous? Do you immediately think of risk to your body, to your savings account, to your job performance, to your relationships, or perhaps to your ego? It's true that some people have a one-sided and limited view of risk taking. They've been led to believe that risk involves danger—perhaps physical danger like the possibility of a car crash from drinking and driving, or emotional danger like the consequences of getting caught cheating. They think that risk is always something to avoid. If you think of risk only in terms of risk protection or risk avoidance, think again. Saying no to risk may be comfortable. It may feel safe. But it's not the way to higher performance.

Whether you define yourself as a risk taker or not, risk is involved in every facet of your life—in your financial affairs, career advancement, professional licensing and education; in your personal life as a spouse, parent and friend; and in your hobbies, fitness activities, creative endeavors, and community outreach.

The terms risk, performance, and success are intertwined and are co-dependent. Risk can be defined as anything you attempt and the outcome is uncertain; success or failure; it works or doesn't work; you look good or you don't look good. There is an element of uncertainty in life—career advancement, relationships, your golf score. All are uncertain, but are worth taking a risk. And there is some degree of anxiety because there are stakes. There could be physical, financial, or emotional jeopardy. Dangerous? Yes! That's what makes life so exciting. I challenge you to take the right risks on purpose. Get a power charge to revitalize the defining factor for achievement and satisfaction: **Purposeful Risk Taking**.

> *Purposeful Risk Taking*
> *means that you understand your*
> *investment, you seek the potential*
> *benefits, and you are willing to stretch*
> *yourself to meet the challenge.*

There's a rhythm to risk taking: Try, fail, try again.

When you were a child you took risks eagerly in order to walk, swing, climb, communicate, read, or make friends. Risking was a necessary component of learning and growing into your potential. It was natural processes of mistake, correction, try again. You held the innate understanding that success was worth the effort. Think about your process as a child to face the risk and challenge of learning to swing. You quickly understood that someone was not always going to be there to push you. Other children seemed to do it with ease. The dilemma: Do you simply sit in the swing, expend no effort, and experience no thrill and sense of accomplishment? Or do you test yourself, expend plenty of energy, pump your legs, and get into the rhythm of swinging?

To experience the thrill of swinging, you had to put effort into learning how to do it on your own. Recall your eagerness to learn and master the challenge. Recollect your resiliency in handling mistakes and failures. Remember your determination to get up and try again. Relive and celebrate your natural risk-taking rhythm.

There is a range of motion in risk taking.

Are you getting everything you can from your swing at life, or do you believe the clichés?

- It's better to be safe than sorry.

- If you can't stand the heat, get out of the kitchen.

- If it ain't broke, don't fix it.

- Don't rock the boat

Have you restricted your own range of motion? That range has been challenged by expectations (your own and others'), peer pressure, fear of failure, and a host of self-limiting clichés and beliefs. Are you limiting your own range of motion? Along life's journey, you undoubtedly have experienced loss, failed relationships, or financial setbacks. Flubs, flops, and failures might have caused you to become risk-shy. No one goes through life unscathed. Loss and failure are a part of life and a part of learning.

When I was between 21 to 31 years old, my father unexpectedly died of a heart attack, I got married, I had three miscarriages, my first house burned to the ground, and my marriage ended in divorce. It was in the reflection on my losses and my failures that I came to truly understand the essence of RISK—the bravery and resiliency that was needed to re-focus my energies, to get back in the swing of life and try again, and to have hope. I resolved then not to give loss and failure the power to limit my range of motion in seeking new opportunities and taking some chances.

Reflect on your life experience as a risk taker. Be honest with yourself.
1. What is the riskiest thing you have ever done?

_____

_____

_____

(...*perhaps getting married, having a child, quitting a job, living abroad, telling off the boss, skinny dipping, bungee jumping?*)

2. What are the risks you would never take?

_____

_____

_____

(...perhaps breaking the law, infidelity, high stakes gambling, drinking and driving, bungee jumping?)

Your answers provide insight into your personal history with risk taking. They help you get a sense of your rhythm and range of motion. And that's the place to begin. Start with thinking about the risks you do take, the risks you won't take, and your attitude towards risk taking.

This book will flip your thinking from the notion of *balance* to the reality of *getting back in the swing* and from the notion of *being* to the reality of *doing the right things*. It will flip your thinking about the concept of risk. It will challenge you to assess whether you are passive or purposeful. It will help you to decide whether your habitual behaviors are sabotaging or supporting you, and it will help you determine whether you are sitting down on the job or in the swing of performing well and making a positive difference in the things that are important to you.

Take a quick accounting. What if you could do the right things to...

- Get learning?

- Get along with people?

- Get healthy?

- Get emotionally fit?

- Get inspired?

Sound good? Then, get back in the swing. These five aptitudes are the gears of effective performance. When you do the right things (like using your resources, adapting to behavioral differences, or maintaining a positive emotional state) you actualize the sensation of effectiveness and worth. You are doing things on purpose to benefit your personal performance and leadership ability.

"Excellence is not a singular act, but a habit. You are what you repeatedly do."

-Shaquille O'Neal

But many people are doing all the wrong things (like bemoaning change, reacting from fear, or hurting others). These behaviors are passive. They are habitual without thinking and without purpose. If you're doing the wrong things, you'll likely pay the price in poor performance, broken relationships, regrets, and/or missed opportunities.

Think about some of your challenges. If you've been resistant to change, felt powerless about influencing others, or been irritable and cranky too often, these are clues that point to passive instead of purposeful risk taking. Habitual, self-defeating behaviors could be sabotaging your abilities. Many people are doing inappropriate, unproductive, even stupid things and not realizing the long-term consequences.

Don't allow yourself to be trapped in bad habits. Don't gamble on your present or future performance. You have a lot to lose. The success you achieve in life depends upon doing the right things in response to the opportunities presented to you. It's not about luck. It's not about age, gender, or social position. It is carefully crafted by what you do every day in your thoughts, actions, and feelings. Five competencies comprise a well-conditioned performance. They are:

- **Innovation:** Research and technology create constant change in information and practice. Learn and grow…or get left in the dust. Rediscover intellectual challenge. Get learning. The payoff is your being smart, prepared, and ready for innovation.

- **Influence:** Build your social capital by accepting others as allies, clarifying how to best interact with them, and creating trust. Get along with other people. Mutually satisfying exchanges with others build continuing influence.

- **Immediacy:** Poor health habits can manifest by illness or obesity. Take care of your body without delay! Get healthy….immediately. Start doing the right things that will improve your health, your sex appeal, and your quality of life.

- **Integrity:** Stressful circumstances or negative people can jolt your emotional stability—if you allow it. Get emotionally fit. Take control of your mood and handle life's challenges with integrity and grace.

- **Inspiration:** There's an energetic spirit needed to take action. It comes from within. Get inspired. Be wild about your performance and growth. Take purposeful risks—intellectually, socially, physically, and emotionally—to lift your self-confidence, enhance your position, and boost your reputation.

Are you investing in these competencies, or are you taking them for granted? Are you passive or purposeful? Most people never reach the level of success of which they are capable because they simply don't challenge themselves to do so. Only those who intentionally engage in improving these competencies will

> *"Risks are a measure of people. People who won't take them are trying to preserve what they have. People who do take them often end up having more."*
>
> -Paul Arden

truly experience it. Stellar achievement never results from inertia; it results from action. This book contains the strategies that will help you take action and do things that matter.

In one of his greatest hits, Duke Ellington crooned these lyrics: *It makes no difference if it's sweet or hot. Just give that rhythm everything you got. It don't mean a thing, if it ain't got that swing.*

Living in Full Swing will put you back in the swing. It will give you some pushes to get you pumping and gliding on your own again. It will help you find your own rhythm and expand your range of motion.

Get ready to exercise your risk-taking muscles for maximizing your competencies. In today's quickly changing and expanding world, the ability to take purposeful risks for positive gain is a valuable asset. RISK IT!

PART I:

Get Learning

CHAPTER 1 | INTELLECTUAL RISK

We live in a brain-based world. New concepts, new technology, and new theories are being developed at lightning speed. Every career field endures a constant blast of innovation, competition and globalization pressures. It's learn and grow, or find yourself left in the dust.

You know this is true, because just when you think you have one thing mastered, what happens? They change it! You master a computer program...they change it. You get comfortable and proficient with a new method of operation...they change it. You finally start to understand the youth lingo...they change it! One of the driving forces of young people is to "talk in code" so adults have no idea what they're talking about. The other day, my nephew was playing a game on a hand-held device.

"Is that your Game Boy?" I asked, showing interest in his activity.

"Oh, Aunt Cathy," retorted my 10-year-old nephew Zachary the whiz kid, "That was so two years ago. This is a PSP." Then with a twinkle in his eyes, he added, "It's just another way for Bill Gates to make more money."

I found out later that PSP stands for Play Station Portable. I admit that I am clueless about the newest electronic devices, games, challenges, and lingo. My nephew smiles with the knowledge that many adults just don't get it, but kids do! And I feel a bit inadequate.

Your brain can do incredible tasks! In addition to rote (facts and studying and tests, oh my!) your amazing brain can:

OBSERVE – *take in information from the senses.*
IMAGINE – *form mental pictures and conceive ideas.*
CREATE – *originate and produce new concepts.*
PREDICT – *figure out what might happen in the future.*
ANALYZE – *separate and examine all the parts.*
MEASURE – *ascertain dimension, quantity or capacity.*
PROBLEM SOLVE – *find solutions and resolve issues.*
DECIDE – *consider options and make choices.*
AS WELL AS *classify, summarize, develop, simplify, agree, compose, elaborate, dispute, assume, prove, prioritize, interpret, compare, contrast, and more......*

So, what does it take to stay up-to-date, resilient, and smart? In his book, *A Celebration of Neurons*, Robert Sylwester reassures us: "The human brain is the best organized, most functional three pounds of matter in the known universe." Small but mighty, it is nature's resource for developing creative responses to any challenge. Evolution has equipped you with curiosity, the natural desire to ask questions, investigate possibilities, and gain knowledge. This ensures that your brain will be loaded with information, skills, and experiences to help you perform to meet the challenge. Your brain empowers you to think, speak, calculate, and write well. It provides the means for you to offer new ideas, build networks, seize opportunities, and/or adapt to change.

But intellectual performance can be risky. And that's a triple whammy:

1. Attempting to learn and master new information or a new skill is a risk. You will succeed, or you will fail in the attempt at learning.

2. Applying that knowledge or skill in real circumstances is a risk. The application will work, or it won't work.

3. Someone will probably be evaluating your proper use of that knowledge or skill! That's risky, too.

Put your brain in reverse and go back to the place in time when you were about fifteen or sixteen years old. Like every other physically able teenager, you were preparing to take the big test to get your driver's license. Test anxiety! Your teenage reputation and popularity were on the line. You were committed to read the manual and study for the written test. You were driven to practice parallel parking, backing up, and stopping right before the stop sign, no matter how far it was from the intersection. You were determined to pass both tests satisfactorily and get your driver's license. It was your passport to freedom, your admittance into teen social life, and your initiation into semi-adulthood. It was the whole triple whammy: study/practice + proper application + evaluation = success or failure. You found the motivation and the persistence to pass the test when you were sixteen. You can still do it.

The concept of learning takes some people right back to elementary school. Facts and studying and tests, oh my!

Much of schoolwork was other-directed, on somebody else's importance list. Mark Twain tells us: *Never let formal education get in the way of your learning.* Optimal learning is self-directed. That means you're in charge. You direct the learning. You open your mind and take the chances. Have no doubt, you do have an awesome brain with an unlimited capacity to learn, grow, and change. Don't be tricked by the saying "You can't teach an old dog new tricks," because every brain has the capacity for lifelong learning. It's just that some people use their brain to perform up to par and some don't. Your daily activities are energized by brain-powered capabilities. Whether you are planning a project, taking step-by-step action, or evaluating progress, your brain is performing.

"The illiterate of the 21st century will not be those who cannot read and write, but those who cannot learn, unlearn, and re-learn."

-*Alvin Toffler*

In what ways could you get more and better intellectual performance from your brain? What do you yearn to do? Do you have verses in your heart, pictures just waiting to be sketched, a new business or product idea formulating in your head? Every day your brain is in action to assist you on many levels: in your profession, in your personal relationships, and in your community involvement.

In this brain-based world, you must have a huge commitment to learning. And that means spending your resources (time, energy, and money) on improving your MIND.

The next ten chapters will give you practical strategies to re-discover intellectual challenge, enhance your lifelong learning, and be ready for innovation. Start learning!

CHAPTER 2 | FIND OUT HOW YOU ARE SMART

*P*eople are "smart" in different ways. Harvard University professor Howard Gardner has identified eight different types of intelligence. Each person is naturally more proficient in some types of smarts than others.

Use this checklist to determine how you are naturally smart. Check any or all that apply to you:

The "HOW Are You Smart?" Checklist
Part 1:

- _ Can you figure correct change, waiter tips, clearance rack percentages into sale price, or batting averages of your favorite baseball players in your head quickly and correctly?

- _ Do you really understand what your financial planner, insurance agent, accountant, stock broker, and car salesperson are saying when they talk numbers?

- _ Can you look at a room and know how to figure the needed amount of paint, carpet, or window blinds? Can you look at a yard or garden and be able to figure the needed amount of grass seed, plants, or fertilizer?

- _ Have you created a workable personal or family budget, do you manage your own bank accounts and investments, or do you know the status of your finances at any given time?

If you can easily do the above types of things, you are probably MATH SMART.

MATH Smart – *the capacity to understand underlying principles of some kind of system and the ability to manipulate numbers. (Logical/Mathematical Intelligence).*

Part 2:

_ Can you easily compose something like a thank-you note, sympathy sentiment, romantic poetry, or clever party invitation at the spur of the moment?

_ Do you find yourself correcting the grammar of other people? Example:

_ Other person: "Where's it at?" Your response: "You mean 'where is it.'

_ Never end a sentence with a preposition." Or correct their spelling? Or correct their punctuation?

_ Do you enjoy reading and discussing books, journal articles, stories, reviews, or editorials? Can you easily express your opinions and ideas to others?

_ Are you the person most likely to write articles for the company newsletter, take minutes at a meeting, create the family Christmas letter, or send a letter to Dr. Phil?

If you can easily do the above types of things, you are probably WORD SMART.

WORD Smart – *the capacity to use language to express what is on your mind and to understand other people. (Verbal/Linguistic Intelligence).*

Part 3:

- _ Do you have the innate ability to keep houseplants living, rose bushes proliferating, or tomato plants yielding produce?

- _ Can you name most of the trees, flowers, grasses, shrubs, or weeds in your yard and garden?

- _ Do you watch birds, talk to animals, keep pets, protect habitats, or feel a natural connection to domestic or wild animals?

- _ Are you naturally curious about the composition of living organisms, the vastness of space or the circle of life?

If you can easily do the above types of things, you are probably NATURE SMART.

NATURE Smart – *the capacity to discriminate among living things as well as sensitivity to other features of the natural world. (Naturalist Intelligence).*

Part 4:

- _ Can you easily pick up a new physical challenge like tai chi, kayaking, or the Texas Two Step?

- _ Can you run, jump, swim, dive, bat, throw, serve, twirl, ski, skate, dance, or any other physical competency with grace and rhythm?

- Do you know how to handle heavy machinery or power tools without hurting yourself or others?

- Do you have the ability to build a deck, sew a dress, construct a computer, or assemble all of your kids Christmas toys correctly?

If you can easily do the above types of things, you are probably BODY SMART.

BODY Smart – *the capacity to use the body or parts of the body (hands, fingers, arms) to solve a problem, make something, or put on a production. (Body/Kinesthetic Intelligence).*

Part 5:

- Can you draw a cartoon, watercolor a landscape, design a quilt pattern, or create a company logo with ease and flair?

- Do you have the ability to assemble a jigsaw puzzle, take great vacation photos, or put together a fabulous outfit?

- Can you quickly figure out a maze; love optical illusions; or see dragons, cathedrals, and your grandma's face in cloud formations?

- Do you doodle on your agenda at meetings, draw pictures on your notepad while talking on the phone, or buy books based solely on the cover design?

If you can easily do the above types of things, you are probably PICTURE SMART.

PICTURE Smart – *the capacity to represent the spatial (actual) world in your mind and being able to communicate it to others. (Visual/Spatial Intelligence).*

Part 6:

_ Do you play the piano, violin, guitar, clarinet, ukulele, or any other musical instrument with dexterity and joy?

_ Can you feel the rhythm in a rain shower, hear the cadence in a train rumbling down the track, tap your foot to the beat of song, or move your body with the tempo of beautiful sounds?

_ Can you compose melodies and lyrics? Do you write "little ditties" and sing them to your kids, your friends, your pets or your plants?

_ Do you lift your voice in joyous song at weddings, funerals, church services, parties, concerts or family gatherings? Do you love to sing?

If you can easily do the above types of things, you are probably MUSIC SMART.

MUSIC Smart – *the capacity to think in music, to be able to hear patterns, recognize them, remember them, and perhaps manipulate them. (Musical/Rhythmic Intelligence).*

Part 7:

_ Do you have the ability to decipher others' behavioral styles and adapt your own style (if needed) to better communicate or work together?

— Can you sense or intuit the needs of others and ask good questions to better understand their position? Are you adept at resolving conflicts and solving problems with your family members, co-workers, or neighbors?

— Do you put effort into being a loving and kind parent, spouse, friend, boss, co-worker, pet owner, or neighbor?

— Do you remember the important people in your life by sending notes, emails, or phone calls of thanks, appreciation, congratulations when appropriate to honor your relationships?

If you can easily do the above types of things, you are probably PEOPLE SMART.

PEOPLE Smart — *the capacity to understand and communicate with other people. (Interpersonal Intelligence).*

Part 8:

— Do you understand your own capabilities and limitations, seek to find new talents (and aren't you still finding talents you never knew you had), and use your gifts to accomplish your mission and give back to the world in service?

— Do you know how and when to motivate yourself? Can you get yourself off the couch and into life? Do you know how to reward your own efforts?

— Can you evaluate your own performance and learn from your mistakes?

_ Do you know what brings you pleasure, how to relax and enjoy life, and how to respect and care for yourself?

If you can easily do the above types of things, you are probably SELF SMART.

SELF Smart – *the capacity to have an understanding of yourself, who you are, and what you can do. (Intrapersonal Intelligence).*

Understanding your natural capacities and limitations makes it easier to see that some learning comes easily and some takes hard work. So which of the above types of intelligence is a match for you? And in which types of intelligence do you struggle?

I am not MATH Smart. Numbers are difficult for me. It was especially troublesome when one of my job expectations as a Wellness and Student Assistance Coordinator for a school district was grant writing. I breezed through the written part but struggled with the budget part. Numbers! It was tedious because I have a tendency to transpose numbers. I had to check and re-check the accuracy of the numbers and the math. It drove me crazy because it was time-consuming and difficult. I would always find the humility to ask the accounting department to review it and make the necessary corrections. Knowing your limitations is important, and asking for assistance takes nothing away from your overall competence.

What matters is your willingness to engage your brain. Learning new information creates new connections in your brain's wiring. Keep practicing and working on your limitations. Reviewing information and performing skills makes those neural networks stronger. As your brain cells become more connected, your brain works more efficiently.

Keep plugging away on your limitations, and remember to celebrate the ways you are naturally smart!

CHAPTER 3 | STAY SHARP AS A TACK

*A*ll brains are created equal. It's just that some people invest in that all-important asset, and some don't. Don't be a slacker. Keep mentally sharp by stimulating your brain cells on a regular basis. Take this quick quiz:

Trivia Quiz

1. In what SPORT is the pennant won?

_____

2. Is page 5 on the right or left leaf of a book?

_____

3. Who wrote the classic *Romeo and Juliet* ?

_____

4. How many stars are in the Big Dipper?

_____

5. Name the capitol city of the state of:

Missouri_____

Florida_____

Maine_____

6. Name the famous boxer played in a movie by actor Will Smith._____

7. Name all the Seven Dwarfs in the Walt Disney movie *Snow White and the Seven Dwarfs*. (Hint: Two names begin with letter D, two with S, and three describe moods or states of being)

_____

_____

_____

In finding the answers to this little quiz, you quickly covered a wide range of information stored in your brain including tidbits in athletics, literature, science, geography, and entertainment. I bet that most of you enjoyed the search-and-find-mission into your brain's information storage tanks.

It is human nature to challenge and test yourself. Your brain likes to work for you. When faced with brain work, thoughts like these frequently pop into your head: *Do I know that? Can I do it? How do I measure up?* You never outgrow the desire for intellectual challenge. Exercise your mind by giving it lots of stimuli.

What? No time, you say? No time for intellectual growth? Haven't you heard? Time is the great equalizer. We all have the same amount of it. How much time do you deplete with habitual time wasters like watching most television shows, playing video games, mindlessly surfing the internet, or fooling with the large percentage of your email or other mail that is useless to you? Einstein proved that time is relative. And time creeps along at a snail's pace when you are bored or impatiently waiting in a line, in traffic, or in a waiting room somewhere.

Trivia Quiz ANSWERS:

1. *Baseball.*
2. *Right.*
3. *William Shakespeare.*
4. *Seven Stars (4 corners of the ladle and 3 in the handle).*
5. *Jefferson City, MO/ Tallahassee, FL./ Augusta, ME.*
6. *Muhammad Ali (or Cassius Clay).*
7. *Doc, Dopey, Sneezy, Sleepy, Bashful, Happy, and Grumpy.*

You do have time for intellectual challenge. Create new things to do during those habitual time-waster segments of your day and during your inevitable waiting time. Engage in conversation with family or friends, work crossword puzzles or word searches, memorize lyrics of a song, play cards, write poetry, learn a new computer program, critique an essay, balance your checkbook, read a good book, stay on top of your financial investments, or learn how to play a PSP with your kids.

"Think left and think right. Think low and think high. Oh the THINKS you can think up if only you try!"

-Dr. Seuss

Stay sharp as a tack. Using your brain will continually stimulate your brain cells and keep your neurons firing. You know the cliché: *Use it or lose it.* This one is true!

CHAPTER 4 | GET MOVING

*T*he works of Paul Dennison in *Brain Gym* and Karla Hannaford in *Smart Moves* demonstrate that you remember things you experience in motion. Motion generates creativity. Motion is emotional. It increases the intensity of feeling about whatever is happening. Movement stimulates blood flow to the brain. It can improve concentration, thinking speed, and organizational skills.

Have you noticed that innovative ideas are often germinated while you are running, swimming, even taking a shower? Do you find yourself standing up to talk on the phone when doing business or discussing problems and walking back and forth across the room? These physical actions—walking, swimming, running, even washing your body in the shower—are cross-lateral movements. Brain researchers report that cross-lateral movement is the synergist for brain activity.

My husband believes that a round of golf is a good example of motion and intellectual activity. He attests that many business deals are closed and partnerships are cemented on the golf course. Perhaps it's because the golf swing (a cross-lateral movement) opens up the brain for thinking and communicating. My husband, Grundy, (yes, that is his real name!), is a retired school principal (though he likes to say he's a "recovering school principal"). When he retired, I knew that I would have to learn to hunt, fish, or play golf...

or be left alone for the rest of my life. I tried all three sporting adventures and believe me, golf is my best shot. Golf is a difficult game, but I am finally getting the swing of it. I enjoy being outside on beautifully manicured golf courses. And the cross-lateral movements of walking and swinging that golf club generate some of my best ideas.

Think of creative ways you can add motion/movement at work or at home to maximize your learning and creativity. Go for a walk and discuss a journal article, problem, or issue with a colleague or family member. Fix a meal together with your family while planning your next vacation or discussing family finances. If you are stuck or have a mental block, get up and walk down the hall or do some stretches. Drawing a problem or topic (cartoons, pictures, symbols) or diagramming all the parts of the issue on a white board provides movement and visual stimulation. Energize your brain by taking notes or doodling on the page during a meeting.

Music can stimulate and exercise your brain, also. The rhythm and beat of a song can enhance neural firing patterns. An upbeat song played before a meeting can have folks bouncing in their seats, causing increased blood flow to the brain. Classical music playing in the background can boost your brainpower. Studies have shown that the complex arrangements in classical tunes can improve thinking and increase attention span.

As I was writing this book, I tried listening to classical music to stimulate my creativity. It usually works for me, but for some reason, it didn't this time. Listening to Elvis did! *Heartbreak Hotel, Blue Suede Shoes,* and *Love Me Tender* from that hunk-a-hunk-of-burning-love was playing in the background. Yep, Elvis was in the house!

Take a chance on some of these motion/learning ideas to better utilize your mind. Use them to help your children enjoy learning too. Think of all the ways you can contribute to your business, family, and organizations by better using the resources of your brain. Add a little movement. Movement stimulates blood flow to the brain, which results in quicker thinking speed and attention to the task at hand.

CHAPTER 5 | CORRAL YOUR RUNAWAY MIND

*I*t is a blessing to live in a time when technological innovations provide instant access to information from all around the world. The benefit is a wealth of knowledge, ideas, and mental stimulation available at your fingertips any time of the day. The frustration is too much information that comes too fast, too frequently, and causes confusion and distraction. Instead of clarity, the barrage of data, facts, statistics, opinions, news, warnings, advice, tips, ads, jokes, lore, and more can be overwhelming. It can impair your ability to focus and be productive.

Technological devices like the laptop and cell phone are designed to be convenient and helpful, but they can provoke a torrent of interruptions. Do machines rule your life? Has TMI (too much info) and techno-mania smashed your attention span? Do you find yourself regularly shifting from one task to another or trying to accomplish several things at once? A 2001 University of Michigan study showed that workers' productivity decreases by 20-40% every time they multitask or task switch. Besides being inefficient and counterproductive, the study also showed that multitasking can lead to short-term memory loss, hypertension, and mental fatigue.

A typical scenario: Maya needs about three hours to write, edit, and polish an important article for the company newsletter. The deadline is 11:30. She begins at 8:00 on the day of her deadline, making this her priority project for the morning. For a short time she thinks about other people in the company who should be writing articles and admonishes them in her mind for their lack of initiative. At 8:30 the phone rings. She checks caller ID and sees that it's a potential client. She vacillates for a few seconds, and then takes the call. She promises to send the requested information by email within the hour. When she sends the email, Maya notices that she has 47 new messages. She scolds herself about not checking emails before she left work last evening. Scrolling through her messages, she quickly deletes 12. She loves the delete key—such immediate satisfaction. She reads five of the most important emails, hoping she remembers to answer them later in the day. Just when she is tempted to click on a pop-up about a free Hawaii vacation, she remembers that deadline. Maya looks at her watch, then wastes several minutes berating herself and agonizing about how little time she has left to prepare. It is 10:00 am. *What happened to the last two hours?*

Interruptions, mental clutter, and the time it took to mentally re-engage each time she made a switch in focus gobbled up those two hours. Sound familiar? Lack of discipline and a runaway mind can steal your productivity.

"Your mind is a tool you can choose to use any way you wish."

-Louise Hay

Take control of your productivity by corralling your runaway mind. Intend to focus. Before you begin an important task that deserves your best, be deliberate about your goal. Make it your intention to give it your full concentration and complete the task. If possible, put your phone on voicemail and ask co-workers or family members for uninterrupted time. Make an agreement with yourself that you will return calls, check emails, and talk with co-workers when this project is complete.

When an unavoidable interruption happens, make the intention that it be brief and efficient. Take care of the business quickly. Then clear your head. Don't let your thoughts ramble. And return to the original task. There is great satisfaction in productivity and the completion of a task. Work done well gives you a sense of personal accomplishment, and an enhanced reputation—and it just might protect you from downsizing, too!

During normal working hours at the office or at home, know that interruptions will occur. Your attention is pulled in many different directions. That's common. Task switching is a part of our lives, but do not allow a runaway mind to steal your productivity. Prepare for increased productivity by refusing to let resistance to an interruption create mishmash in your mind. Thoughts such as mentally scolding the person who interrupts you, agonizing over lost time, berating yourself, or poor-me-ism are unhelpful and a waste of time. If your thoughts take off in a negative direction, remind your brain to re-engage in the task. Discipline your mind and take charge of your thoughts. It can reduce the time between tasks. It can also make you a happier and more productive person.

Learn to finish one thing before you start something else. If an interruption produces another task you need to accomplish, write it down so you don't forget. But finish the first task. Constant task-switching can induce frustration and that familiar "I didn't get anything done!" feeling. Always give your brain this message: *Intend to focus.* The intention will give you positive energy for focused spurts of productivity and disciplined thoughts. It is all a mental game.

CHAPTER 6 | CLAIM CHANGE

*H*ave you tried anything new lately? If given the opportunity to try something new right now such as learning a new technique that would help you work more productively, would you:

- Jump at the chance to be first?

- Wait until someone else tried it, then attempt it?

- Have to be pushed and prodded to try anything new?

Many people are resistant to anything new or different. They cling to the status quo. The unpredictability of change or challenge causes them instant anxiety, so they slam the door on opportunity and put out the "Do not disturb" sign.

Anxiety. Sometimes it's a flicker of uneasiness in the back of your mind. Other times it is a shock wave of dread over your entire body. At times, it saves you. And at times, it shuts you down. There are many situations in which change—a modification, replacement, transformation, or something new and different in your immediate environment, can cause anxiety. Anxiety prompts a person to say things like: *I can't do this. I don't know how. I won't change. It's too risky. I'm not a good learner, a good adapter, or a good sport either! Don't make me do this.*

Joan was in a teambuilding workshop I was facilitating with an administrative team of about 30 people. During the morning session, we celebrated their individual behavioral styles and delved into ways they could adapt to each other to be more productive. In the afternoon session, we tackled some changes that the team would be facing and explored techniques for successfully implementing the new procedures. I noticed that Joan's demeanor had changed in the afternoon. She became unresponsive and closed. At a break, I approached her and asked if she had any concerns to share with me.

"I'm not in this job for personal success or team camaraderie," she blurted. "I just want to do my job and go home."

After some gentle probing, I discovered that Joan was confusing anxiety about the upcoming changes with anxiety about the teambuilding process. She admitted that she was rejecting change— not her co-workers or her job success. She felt apprehensive and incompetent because of the new procedures. Her brave admission freed her mind and enabled her to focus on what was needed for change.

When opportunity (probably in the form of change) knocks, don't impulsively reject it. Open the door. Face it. Circle around it. Scan it with all of your senses. Look, hear, feel, smell, taste it. Go to your intuition for a gut feeling. Identify what makes you fearful or uneasy. Process your thoughts and feelings. Look for the benefits, or the WIIFM (What's In It For Me). And remember that you are a talented, resourceful, and creative person with a brain. Then resolve to give it a try.

With something new, whether it's learning a new computer program or swinging a nine iron, everyone starts on square one at the beginning with the first attempt. You must risk being a beginner. It is uncomfortable to be a beginner. You might feel embarrassed and self-conscious. There most likely will be goofs, do-overs, and miscues. Sometimes it takes a few attempts to get it right. Sometimes it takes a lot of practice and effort.

You always have a choice: 1) Give up, or 2) Claim that change, get up, and try again. It is your choice. Claim that change. Give yourself a chance and do it again. Persist through the beginner's feelings of uncertainty, incompetence, and frustration. Then do it again and again if necessary until you do it right or get better at it.

You can't dodge change! There's no escape. The opportunities for change presented to you are life's way of telling you it's time for you to update, alter your direction, learn new skills, or transform yourself. So claim it. It's time to do something new or different....and become better, more modernized, or more accomplished.

CHAPTER 7 | BAIL, WAIL, OR FAIL

"*B*ut," you might be thinking, "what if the change is my idea? What if I want to suggest an alternative, a split-up, a brilliant new concept, or a big reorganization plan?"

In that case, you do face possible disappointment. You might lose face. Your co-workers, friends, or family members might think you're crazy. They might reject your proposal. They might think less of you. They might be threatened and resentful of your possible success. Yikes! Will you bail, wail, or go for it...even if you might fail?

> "*I fail my way to success.*"
>
> -*Thomas Edison*

If you want success or you want things to be different, you have to be prepared for failure. And you will fail at times...in relationships, job promotions, financial investments, contests, elections, or many other endeavors. Failure is just as likely an outcome as success. An Old West cowboy saying declares: *There never was a horse that couldn't be rode and there never was a rider that couldn't be throwed.*

Be willing to experience all of life—the ups and the downs—and learn from mistakes and failure. View setbacks as lessons learned. Each lesson is another step forward.

Failure builds brainpower. It forces you to use your gray matter and sharpen your thinking skills.

- Clarification: What worked and what didn't work?

- Creativity: What other options are there?

- Critical Thinking: What can I learn from this?

- Calculation: What is the worst that could happen and how would I handle it?

Some people face failure, and bail. Some wail and find excuses for poor performance, becoming bitter and negative. And some face the same failure and try again, becoming stronger, more determined, and mentally tougher. What's the difference? It is all in how you view the risk of success or failure. Is it challenging or threatening? Are you resilient? Can you find your mistake-correction, try-again rhythm? Can you get back in the swing and keep trying?

Director/actor Woody Allen reminds us: *Failure is a sure sign that you're not playing it safe, that you're still experimenting, still taking creative risks....If you're succeeding too much, you're doing something wrong.*

Whether your attempt at something new is unsolicited, forced or chosen, view it as an opportunity for personal growth and expanding your assets. If *Better to be safe than sorry* keeps popping into your head, remember that you are not designed to play it safe. You are designed for performance. It's what your body, brain, and voice are made for. Claim that change and do it....again, again, and again.

CHAPTER 8 | FIGURE YOUR HANDICAP

*M*any of my friends and family members are banking and paying their bills on-line. They have explained the benefits and encouraged me to do the same thing. Each time someone sings the praises of sending money through air, I listen, amazed. I realize that it is a quicker, more efficient process. I know that banking this way saves money for postage, but I just haven't tried it yet. What's wrong with me?

Of course, it is human nature to want things to stay the same. Change-resistance is fueled by three learning handicaps:

- **Not knowing:** You need to *know* that the change adds value, improves quality or productivity, increases motivation and morale, or encourages innovation. You need to *know* the benefits. How will things will be better if you make a change?

- **Not able:** You need to be *able* to do what's required. You need to have the knowledge or skills. You need to have the right tools or technology and be *able* to use them. Ability has a profound effect on cooperation, and skills build confidence.

- **Not willing:** You need to be *willing* to try the new approach, put in the time and effort, be coached and receive feedback. You need to be *willing* to take the risk.

This is attitude. You move yourself past the *I can't, don't want to, can't make me* attitude into the *Okay, I'll give it try* attitude.

You've probably heard the phrase: *The only difference between TRY and TRIUMPH is just a little UMPH.* The UMPH is time and effort. In our busy, over-scheduled, fast-paced lifestyles, time and effort are at a premium.

I evaluated my situation with the on-line banking to figure my handicap. Number one, check. I know the benefits. Number two, check. I have a computer and am able to use it. Number three. Now that's the kicker. I am just not willing to take the time and effort to figure it out right now or to ask one of my friends or family members to show me how to do it. So I am stuck doing it the same old way. Funny, isn't it? I can't seem to make the time for something that could save me both time and money. Fortunately for me, there is no pressure from someone else to conform to the new way. But I now know my handicap and I can make a plan to help me accomplish the change.

Whatever change or challenge you face, put yourself and your situation under the same scrutiny. Figure your handicap.

1. Do you know the benefits?

If not, ask others, read up on it, or do an internet search. Re-frame your thinking to look for the positive aspects instead of excuses, drawbacks or reasons for not changing.

2. **Are you able to do it with your knowledge, skills, and tools?**

If not, seek the proper training and equipment. Take a class. Listen to audio tapes. Get coaching or mentoring. Resolve to make the change.

3. **Are you willing to put in the time and effort required to make the change?**

If not, determine the costs, damages, or reparations of your inaction. Look at what you have to lose if you are not willing to do it. Determine to take the risk and take action.

> *"Unless you try to do something beyond what you have already mastered, you will never grow."*
>
> -Ralph Waldo Emerson

Even if you feel you are being forced into a change that you don't want, there is power in being able to interpret your own struggle. Remember that all learning is change. You change from a state of not knowing to a state of knowing. Understanding your change-resistance learning handicaps can help you put your thoughts and feelings in order. It can help you make a plan to positively deal with the change. Now, that is using your head.

CHAPTER 9 | FACE YOUR SNAKES

One Saturday morning in the spring, my husband was on the golf course with his golf buddies. I was getting ready to do the week's laundry. I picked up the laundry basket and took it down to the basement.

"I have accepted fear as a part of life—specifically the fear of change.... I have gone ahead despite the pounding in the heart that says: turn back."

-Erica Jong

Well, not really a basement. It was more like a cellar. We were living in a 100-year-old farmhouse in the country that we had totally remodeled, except for the cellar. It had rock foundation walls on three sides. But on the fourth wall, behind the washer and dryer, the rocks went up only three-fourths of the way (about eye level for me), leaving an opening to the crawl space under the rest of the old house. The crawl space was dark, dank, cobwebby, and creepy. I had conditioned myself to ignore it.

This particular morning, I put the basket down in front of the washing machine and reached for the soap. At that moment my ears heard a slight sliding sound, my peripheral vision picked up movement, and I whipped around to be eyeball to eyeball with a five-foot-long **black snake** sliding across the top of the rock wall behind the washing machine. In a split second, I raced up the steps, slammed the door, locked it, and spent the next two or three hours in a tizzy. A snake in my basement! I was beside myself. I didn't get a thing done all morning except call my mother, and it was the first time *ever* that my Mom was at a loss to tell me what to do!

When my husband returned from the golf course, I pounced on him as swiftly as a snake striking its prey. I wanted him to get that snake out of the basement immediately. Grundy grew up on a farm and he realized that this was my first experience with country living, so he began the patient process of breaking down my bias and fear of snakes. He didn't laugh at me or make fun of my fear, but he explained to me why farmers actually *like* black snakes.

"Cathy, black snakes are good snakes," he explained.

"There is no such thing as a good snake," I interrupted.

"Honey," he persisted, "they eat rodents who cause damage by eating farmers' grain, carrying disease, and chewing through wood and wiring. Black snakes don't do any damage or carry disease. They are reclusive, mind their own business, and usually avoid contact with people. They are harmless."

My husband assured me that, because of our extensive remodeling efforts, there were no holes or openings from the basement and the snake could not get into the house.

"Better to have a snake in the crawl space than mice," he propositioned. "The snake can probably get in and out of the crawl space under the house and will eat any nasty little mice that might be there, too."

He even went to the bookstore and purchased a book on snakes. The chapter on black snakes reinforced what he had told me. Believe it or not, he convinced me to leave the black snake alone. My frantic level of anxiety was diminished because of my husband's empathy and appropriate information about the snake.

So I named the snake "Blackie" and I guess it lived in the crawl space. Every time I had to go down to the basement to do the laundry, I banged on the door and told Blackie to hide. I only saw that snake three more times in the six years we lived there. I was jumpy when I saw it, but no longer fearful. I understood that there was nothing to fear from a black snake.

The brain is well-equipped to register the feelings of fear, anxiety, and worry. Our survival instinct allows us to anticipate danger and to take action to prevent it. This is valid fear and is essential to our well-being. As a speaker, I frequently experience a tinge of fear and anxiety if I am presenting a new topic or to a new type of audience. This is a valid fear that motivates me to question and learn as much as I can about the situation, the setting, the audience, and the topic in order to be properly prepared and do my best.

Lack of information and preconceived bias can cause excessive anxiety, impair judgment, and hinder achievement. The key is confronting your personal biases and learning more about the situation or the thing you fear. In his book *Chancing It*, Ralph Keyes says that *Risk is in the fears of the beholder.*

There are big fears: fear of death, losing someone you love, cancer, or financial ruin. There are common fears: fear of falling on your face, being laughed at, being rejected, or looking stupid. Finally, there are individual fears: scary things that lurk in your own subconscious, like my fear of the black snake. Face your snakes and learn more about them.

I find it interesting that the snake represents change, transformation, shedding the old, and rebirth. The snake is an ancient symbol of healing. I'll always remember that black snake in my basement as a lesson about appropriately handling fear with information and objectivity. We've since moved from that old house back to the farm in Platte County, MO, on which my husband was raised. We have built a beautiful new house on this farm. But guess who's living in our big old red barn? Another Blackie!

CHAPTER 10 | TUG ON YOUR BRAIN

*H*ave you ever been stumped or stymied by a question? Baffled or bewildered by an obstacle? Confounded or confused by an unexpected situation? Most of the time your brain does a fine job of confronting the challenge and filtering through your knowledge, experience, and skills to create solutions for you to try. Your brain will enlist thoughtful guessing strategies, and it will be imaginative and curious.

Sometimes you might keep thinking: *Curiosity killed the cat.* Sometimes you might not trust your own capabilities. Sometimes you might give up way too soon. Sometimes you might get stuck thinking that there is only one right answer.

Our financial planner is named Tim. In our yearly review meeting, Tim shared a concern about his first child, a 10-month-old little girl named Jordan. He and his wife were worried because Jordan was not crawling yet. Not crawling, not rolling, not scooting on her belly, not sliding across the floor—just sitting. That's all Jordan did. Tim and his wife would get down on the floor and demonstrate appropriate 10-month-old types of moving around. But Jordan merely watched them and giggled or gooed.

"One day I had a bright idea," Tim exclaimed. "Her favorite snack is dry cereal. So I put a blanket on the floor, sat her on one corner of the blanket, and put a pile of cereal on the opposite corner of the blanket. I got down on the floor with Jordan and demonstrated how to crawl to the other corner of the blanket to eat the cereal."

Just the thought of an adult male crawling across the floor to eat cereal on the floor made me laugh. "Well, did it work?" I asked.

"No," he smiled. "Jordan just gave me a puzzled look then simply picked up the edge of the blanket and pulled the corner with the cereal to her!"

Smart baby. She didn't have the skills to crawl yet, the only solution that had been modeled for her. But she wanted the cereal. She couldn't get to it. So her inventive brain created another option, one that surprised her parents. She tugged on the blanket till she dragged that cereal to her. That's creative solution finding from a 10-month-old child.

Your brain loves a challenge. It is designed to link, loop, and connect ideas—that is, if you let it do its job. It is easy to let initial thoughts—*I can't crawl; It can't be done; It won't work; So why try; If it ain't broke, why fix it*—close your mind.

In what ways have you shut yourself down? Limited your abilities? Shackled your brain? Tied your own hands?

Train yourself to recognize negative or restrictive thoughts and immediately let them go. Push them out of your brain. Once you open your mind and trust your brain, solutions and ideas will pour out.

Ask yourself good questions to stimulate even better ideas. *Can I do it faster? Can I do it smarter? Can I do it better? Can I have more fun doing it?* Have confidence in your ability to learn, create, adapt, and invent. Enjoy the process. Let your brain work for you. I'll bet you can come up with your own "tug on the blanket" solutions. Just tug on your brain and it will work for you.

CHAPTER 11 | SWING AWAY

It was a classic moment. The score was 4 to 6. It was the bottom of the last inning, two runners on base, and there were two outs. The high school state championship in baseball was on the line. The big guy was up to bat. He was the team's strongest hitter with eight home runs for the season going into the game. But during this championship game, he had been at the plate three times and had struck out three times! All eyes in the stadium were on him at the moment. The outcome of the game depended on his performance. Could he get a hit? Would they walk him on purpose since he was a potentially powerful hitter? Or would he stay in the slump and strike out again? Can't you just imagine the pressure this young man was under?

He took a deep breath, looked at the third base coach, and nodded. He stepped into the batter's box. He let the first pitch go by. The umpire called a strike and the fans groaned. On the second pitch, with one confident swing, he knocked the ball right out of the stadium, winning the game with a three-run home run!

What a performance! I was there. My brother Dan was the coach of the 1991 high school state championship team. Dan said (of course), "It was simply good coaching. I gave him the home run sign!" *Right!*

There is a price to pay for successful performance. That price is training your mind to be persistent, to learn from your mistakes, and to keep trying. Achievement is rooted squarely in how often you try. It's quantity. The great home run hitters in any field—athletes, scientists, inventors, artists, authors, designers, entrepreneurs, and investors—all had many failures for every single success. They made many attempts. It takes ideas, more ideas, and even more ideas to get the one big home run idea. And it takes attempts at performance, more attempts at performance, and even more attempts at performance to achieve the home run performance.

Swinging away tests your endurance. It takes courage to put your ideas and your skills on the line multiple times. It takes resiliency to bounce back and regroup your efforts when you strike out. It takes persistence. But quantity produces quality. Swing away.

Don't wait for opportunity to knock. Seek it out. Frank Scully said it best: *Why go out on a limb? Isn't that where the fruit is?* There is always something new to see, hear, taste, smell, touch, or experience. There are opportunities for expansion all around you. Most people never pursue new knowledge or skills outside of what is required to keep their jobs. With a ready supply of new and interesting information, you can become a better worker, boss, parent, spouse, friend, athlete, or hobby enthusiast. Enriching your mind with new ideas or skills will enrich your life with knowledge, wisdom, and experience. All learning leads to a B-I-G payoff. You become smart, prepared, and ready for innovation.

SWING AWAY!

Use these action verbs to jumpstart your intellectual performance.

1. **Explore**   Venture out and explore a local flea market, the woods nearby, or a new internet site. Go on a field trip. Travel to sites around town, off the beaten path, or to exotic places. The desire to learn requires inspiration.

What do you want to explore?

_____

_____

_____

_____

_____

_____

2. **Read**   Books can take you on wonderful adventures to learn about places, cultures, situations, events, people, and philosophies. Creative or critical thinking requires an influx of new ideas, attitudes, themes, and sparks.

What do you need to read?

_____

_____

_____

_____

_____

3. Study   This is not a school word. It is a life word. The mind is a terrible thing to waste. Take a class and study an interesting subject. Go shopping to study prices and value. Write in a journal and study the twists and turns of your own life. Understanding requires knowledge of facts.

What would you like to study?

_____

_____

_____

_____

_____

_____

4. Practice   Tony Robbins, motivational speaker and author, says: *Repetition is the mother of skill.* Success requires practice. Practice the skills of a sport, the creativity of writing, the techniques of conflict resolution, the art of pie making, or the craft of compassion. Successful performance requires mastery of skills.

What do you want to practice?

_____

_____

_____

_____

_____

_____

5. Experiment   Have the courage to try a different haircut, a new restaurant, a new type of volunteerism, a new technique, or a fresh view. Look at things differently and put ideas together in an unconventional way.

How can you experiment with something new?

_____

_____

_____

_____

_____

CHAPTER 12 | REACH NEW HEIGHTS

*"You may be disap-
pointed in you fail,
but you are doomed
if you don't try."*

-Beverly Sills

There is no one-size-fits-all plan for intellectual performance. You need to evaluate your intentions for learning and personal growth. How can you improve? Are there changes that need your attention? How can you better perform your job or role responsibilities? What do you want to explore, read, study, practice, or experiment? What do you need to un-do, re-do, do-over or just **do**? As you think about how you want to improve your intellectual performance, keep in mind the purpose of intellectual risk taking: to proactively gain knowledge, skills, and experience for better performance; to find ways to better use your talents and abilities; to develop your resourcefulness, creativity, and innovative thinking; and to adapt to change or be change-ready.

Sometimes all you need is a little push to get you pumping and gliding on your own. Get learning. Here is a quick reminder of the ten incentives in this section to get you back in the swing of innovation:

- **Find Out How Smart You Are:** Celebrate your natural strengths and work on your limitations.

- **Stay Sharp as a Tack:** Exercise your brain with lots of stimuli.

- **Get Moving:** Add movement to stimulate quicker thinking speed and attention to the task.

- **Corral the Runaway Mind:** Manage task switching and improve productivity.

- **Claim Change:** See change as an opportunity for growth and improvement.

- **Bail, Wail, or Fail:** Be prepared for failure.

- **Figure Your Handicap:** Analyze your change-resistant handicaps.

- **Face Your Snakes:** Learn more about situations you fear.

- **Tug on Your Brain:** Release your self-limiting beliefs and trust your brain.

- **Swing Away:** Go for quantity to get home run ideas and performances.

Incorporating these habits into your intellectual performance can help you reach new heights in INNOVATION.....Risk it!

PART II:

influence

Get Along With People

CHAPTER 13 | SOCIAL RISK

*P*erforming effectively in relationships requires finesse in people skills.

"I suppose leadership at one time meant muscles, but today it means getting along with people."
-Indira Gandhi

Peter Drucker, well-known business management theorist, (who passed away in November 2005 at the age of 95!), coined the name *social capital*, defined as the sum value (number + depth + quality) of your relationships. Although the last thirty years of the world were dominated by economic capital, Drucker predicted that the next thirty years will be driven by social capital. When you read the newspaper or listen to the news on television, you realize that all people have major relationship problems. The inability to build and sustain social capital is responsible for our greatest fears: terrorism, war, violence, and abuse. The future will be driven by the way people behave or feel toward each other and the way they work together and combine forces. What influence will you have?

Influence is your competence in building social capital. It is your power to produce positive effects on the actions or thoughts of other people. Serving customers, selling, partnering, mentoring, networking, alliance building, making friends, and even parenting are all components of social capital. Whether they are above you, below you, or on the same step in the pecking order, other people can add so much to life. These people can lift you up, make you feel appreciated, and infuse you with positive energy.

It seems so natural to form good relationships, but the ability to get along with others is not something you are born with. It's something you have to learn. You learned how to "play nice" in the back yard, how to listen and respond in the classroom, and how to love and be loved in the family room. Influencing others while making them feel honored and secure is risky business. It's social risk taking. The risk is that trust and openness won't be returned or might be misinterpreted. If you can shift the focus from your own interpersonal frustrations to better understanding and satisfying the needs of others, you will greatly increase your social capital. The following eight chapters provide practical strategies for recognizing common relationship mistakes, correcting your errors, and increasing your influence.

CHAPTER 14 | SIZE UP YOUR ALLIANCES

*I*t is human nature to size up others to see if they might be potential opponents, competitors, allies, or friends. You might sense that a new co-worker might change the dynamics of the office. A new neighbor could be a nuisance. Your daughter's new boyfriend might threaten your family's stability. Creating a new relationship as well as maintaining established relationships starts with how you **think** about that other person.

If you think that they are a threat in some way, it will be difficult to build mutual trust. Don't immediately draw the battle lines. That only creates tension. No matter how unhappy you might be about the circumstances of a relationship, you must begin by thinking of that person as an ally.

To jump-start the process of alliance-thinking, first consider the mission or goal you have in common: for instance a good working environment, a peaceful neighborhood, or keeping your daughter happy and safe. Defining the mutual goal helps you size that person up as part of an alliance. If the word "ally" isn't a fit for you, you can substitute helper, colleague, or associate. It is absolutely necessary to see the other person from a neutral position as a stakeholder with a shared mission.

Allow that person to contribute to the common goal by sharing their skills and expertise. This is a mindset too.

Take the position of allowing or permitting him or her to be true to self. People are most content when they are using their talents. If they realize that you appreciate what they have to share and support their efforts, they will be more willing to cooperate. Competition or conflict might flare up, and it should be resolved (tips in a later chapter). But always return your focus to the position of allowing your ally to contribute.

Train your mind to think in this equation:

Your contribution + ally contribution
= alliance to achieve mutual goal.

CHAPTER 15 | START TALKING

*I*n the past, you might have heard a teacher or parent say: "Stop talking and get to work." That advice is appropriate some of the time, like when you need to reflect and think. But just as often, the advice should be: "Start talking and get to work."

Research shows that your brain is a social organ. It likes to talk. It takes pleasure from listening and connecting with people. It delights in formulating, linking, and sharing ideas. Having good social skills is necessary both in business and in personal success, from the boardroom to the family room. The trouble is that currently we have less practice in talking to others because of garage door openers, caller ID, automated phone systems, email, online chat rooms, internet shopping, and drive-through— everything from fast food to pharmacies to dry cleaners. Conversing with others is a critical skill in creating influence. People need opportunities to practice talking with others.

When I was in school, one of the regular assignments was rote memorization of quotations, poems, excerpts, dates, and facts. One of the assignments that I did retain is this snippet by the poet Rudyard Kipling: *I had six honest, serving men. They taught me all I knew. Their names were What and Where and When and Why and How and Who.*

His "honest, serving men" are the six starter words for questions. Good questions allow you to start and continue meaningful interaction. Questioning savvy can be used to engage others in order to obtain information, clarify misunderstandings, and assess progress.

Questioning Savvy

- **Obtain information:**

How do you see the problem?
Who else is involved?
Why are we/you doing it this way?
Who/What will be affected?

- **Clarify differences:**

Are we moving too quickly?
Can you work within this structure?
What are you thinking/feeling?
Do you agree/disagree?

- **Assess progress:**

Who is getting results?
When can I expect the details?
How will we/you know if this plan works?
Do you need assistance?

You can adapt these types of questions to suit your situation whether it is interaction with your children, spouse, neighbors, co-workers, or your boss. Asking good questions then really listening to what the other person says shows that you are interested in them, you respect their thoughts and feelings, and you care about them. In Stephen Covey's book, *7 Habits of Highly Effective People,* one of Stephen Covey's habits is: *Seek first to understand, then be understood.* When people feel heard, they are more inclined to share real, honest feedback. Best of all, it gives you clues for understanding their operating system. When you are aware of the differences in thinking, you then have the power to mesh ideas and achieve compatibility.

MENTORING

A mentor is a person, usually more experienced, who develops a one-to-one relationship with a learner who wants to grow personally or professionally. Mentoring is the act of providing guidance, encouragement, support and positive example to someone else.

The concept of mentoring goes back in history to Greek mythology. In Homer's Odyssey, Mentor was the teacher of Odysseus's son. Mentor was half-man and half-woman. Throughout history, the mentoring tradition has been used in craft apprenticeships and work "buddy" arrangements for knowledge and skill building.

Start talking and get to work. Expand your social networks by joining a professional organization or club, creating a mastermind group, mentoring someone, joining a book club, volunteering in a church or community service project, taking a class, or talking to your family members more often. In every social situation, hone your ability to communicate with your co-workers and family members. Ask interesting questions. Listen for understanding.

The ability to ask good questions can cement relationships, create a positive work and home culture.... and maybe even give birth to world peace!

CHAPTER 16 | LOOK, LISTEN, AND LEARN

*H*ave you ever been blindsided by a clash of behavioral styles? It happened to me one September. My job as an educator had been restructured. My teaching load was reduced to four morning classes and my afternoons were now devoted to an administrative district assignment. In the process, I gained an office and lost a classroom. That meant being a "traveling teacher" and using a different teacher's classroom during their plan time for my morning classes. No one likes this situation, but sometimes it is inevitable.

Before school started, I had a quick visit with each teacher, looked at their classrooms, and asked questions about the room and procedures. School started and everything went okay. Hectic, but okay. *Or so I thought.* It turned out that things were fine with three of the teachers whose rooms I used, but not with one. I didn't realize it for weeks, but he was very upset with me. My behavioral style and teaching methods were different from his. I used cooperative learning techniques and frequently moved the desks around. My classes did projects, demonstrations, and productions with props that students brought into his room (my room for one period of the day) in the morning and needed some place to put them. He filled the chalkboards each day with notes and assignments, leaving me no room. Sometimes I would erase his instructions, write mine, and then hurriedly replace his at the end of the hour. I don't have very neat penmanship.

He did. He finally became so upset that he started telling other teachers and students that he was irritated with me. And of course, they told me.

We both learned a big lesson that September. We discovered how to look, listen, and learn. We discovered the importance of being aware of and adapting to each other's behavioral style. We listened to each other's concerns, realized our behavioral differences, and looked for options and solutions that we could both live with. We came to the understanding that we were different, but it was okay to have different styles. The key was our willingness to adapt so we could get along.

Any time you work with other people, whether on a committee or task force at work, church, neighborhood, or community, you make three deals:

1. You agree on a common goal.

2. You agree to share your time, talents and resources to achieve the goal.

3. You agree to work together.

Deal #3 is the difficult part because, most of the time, you don't get to choose your co-workers, managers, or teammates. Before you can communicate well with them, you have to develop an understanding of their behavioral styles. Your behavior style creates the filters through which you perceive and react to stimuli. Do you understand your own behavioral style? Take this quick assessment:

Either...Or

Choose one statement in each of the following categories that best suits your behavioral style:

COMPETITION...

_____I thrive on competition!	_____I am intimidated by competition.

CONFLICT...

_____In response to conflict, I tend to confront, argue or negotiate.	_____In response to conflict, I tend to avoid or compromise.

IDEAS...

_____I get jazzed by taking one idea and making it work.	_____I get jazzed by creating lots of ideas.

TIME MANAGEMENT...

_____When I have much to do, I save the most pleasant tasks for last.	_____When I have much to do, I begin with the most pleasant tasks.

PRESSURE...

_____Give me deadlines, I work BEST under pressure.	_____Don't give me deadlines, I CLUTCH under pressure.

You have your own special way of perceiving and reacting to these situations based on your past experience, opinions, preferences, and habits. The way you face these conditions is unique to you. You know exactly where you stand on these issues. In any one of the above categories, if you checked the response on the left side, there are many others who would check the right side. And the person responding differently from you can drive you crazy with that reaction! For instance, I always save the most pleasant tasks for last. My brain is hardwired to get the difficult and lousy things out of the way first and then enjoy the pleasurable tasks last as a reward. It makes me crazy when I see other people doing the fun things first. It's just not right. My error is in thinking that everyone else should think, feel, and behave the same way I do.

Behavioral style is your innate reaction to the circumstances of life and your manner of conducting yourself. People react differently to the circumstances of relationships:

- **Social interaction:** Some are extroverts (get energy from people) and some are introverts (get energy from self).

- **Problem solving:** Some are doers and want to take action immediately; others are thinkers and need time for processing.

- **Level of action:** Some need a quick, energetic tempo of activity; others prefer an unhurried and deliberate pace.

- **Organization:** Some need specific structure and procedures to be followed; some feel confined by too much structure and want to do things their own way.

> *"If a man does not keep pace with his companions, perhaps it is because he hears a different drummer. Let him step to the music he hears, however measured or far away."*
>
> *-Thoreau*

There is no right or wrong response in these differences. People have their own hardwired propensity for behaving. Error correction requires an awareness of these differences and the ability to adapt when needed. You can discover yours and others' behavioral styles by being aware of the variances, paying attention, observing behavior, and asking questions to check for understanding. Look, listen, and learn. Then honor yourself. You're okay the way you are. And honor your ally. He's okay too—different, but okay.

CHAPTER 17 | BUILD TRUST

*S*olitary confinement is considered to be the worst form of punishment. We need people. But sometimes, relationships can be so perplexing and generate a torrent of questions in your mind: *Who's the boss? Where's the power? What's the purpose? Can I trust you? Who profits from this? Who is to blame? What about my needs? Will you love me in the morning?*

Many people today tell us that strength is in independence. *Believe only in yourself and you won't be hurt or misled. Trust is unnecessary and caring is weakness. Be strong.*

The paradox is that humans have a deep need for connections with other people. We make friendships, join churches, sign up for committees, and create families. All good relationships, whether business or personal, demand trust and caring on some level. Being hurt is sometimes an unfortunate outcome of relationships. It is the risk you take when you become involved with others. Each encounter with another person has an energy charge. Whether the energy charge is positive or negative depends upon your response to the situation. Your response has a positive or negative effect on the connection.

Look at the Energy Chart on page 86. The middle column displays a list of situations with the heading **Common Interactions**. These situations represent normal everyday occurrences between people. If you haven't learned to create

ENERGY CHART

Connect	Common Interactions	Disconnect
Approval *Asking* *Appreciation*	← **Enlisting HELP from others** →	*Guilt* *Demanding* *Threats*
Assuming *responsibility* *Focus: solutions*	← **Dealing with CONFLICT** →	*Avoidance* *Backstabbing* *Fighting*
Listening *Asking questions* *Making changes*	← **Reacting to CRITICISM** →	*Fear* *Defensiveness* *Denial*
Feedback *Assistance* *Reinforcement*	← **Evaluating PERFORMANCE** →	*Sarcasm* *Withholding* *reinforcement*
Listening *Acceptance* *Support*	← **Sharing IDEAS** →	*Mockery* *Cold stares* *Put downs*
Being kind *Being firm* *Assertiveness*	← **Handling INTERRUPTIONS** →	*Anger* *Attacking* *Withdrawal*

↓ **CARING**   ↓ **SELFISH**

a positive energy charge that connects with people, these situations can turn into stink bombs and ruin your relationships!

Please review the responses in the right hand column under the heading **Disconnect**. To some of them, I can hear your reaction: *Ummm, guilty.* Me, too. These reactive responses represent your primary defense mechanism, or your unconscious method of getting your own way. This defense mechanism roots in fear, ego, and control. These behaviors are so easy because they're driven by self-gratification. They're indulgent, intemperate, and selfish. The backlash, however, is that they cause internal stress and negative energy. People are generally blind to their own bad behavior. But remember that bad behavior results in a "disconnect" in the relationship bond.

Now, scan the responses in the left-hand column with the heading **Connect**. Here there is a conscious attempt for mutual understanding and creating win/win solutions. I admit that this kind of behavior (like all good things) takes effort. It roots in love. Love is the universal force that calls you to be a better person and to act purposefully from caring, compassion, and peace. There is an entirely different feel here. These replies create positive energy. Caring actions build trust. Caring actions "connect" people.

Great tension exists between your selfish ego and your caring nature. The demanding ego speaks loudly. If you find that some of your immediate reactions come from the **Disconnect** column of the chart, you need to correct those mistakes and change your habits. It is a big risk to change your behavior from selfish to caring. You have to rebuild mental muscles and train your brain to think and act from a loving perspective. I saw this slogan on a church sign recently: *No act of love is ever wasted.* How inspiring!

Each day, each hour, with each interaction, you are choosing between connection or disconnection, between love or ego, between positive energy or negative energy. You'll know whether or not you have made the right choice by the other person's reaction. Negative energy will not win friends and influence people; positive action will nurture others, make them feel good, and nudge them to be a better person.

"Do what's right! Do the best you can and treat others the way you want to be treated because they will ask three questions: 1) Can I trust you? 2) Are you committed? 3) Do you care about me as a person?"

-Lou Holz

Remember the Universal Law of Attraction: *Like attracts like.* What you put out will come back to you. I read an article in my local Platte City, MO, newspaper about the Christmas Day 2004 earthquake off the west coast of Northern Sumatra which caused the deadly tsunami. The article states that according to the Department of Natural Resources, shortly after the magnitude 9.0 quake rocked the Far East, shock waves reached as far away as Missouri, causing fluctuations in groundwater levels in observation wells. In the same vein, you'll never know the outreach of your actions, how far they will travel, who they will touch. Your outflow of words and actions are comparable to a pebble tossed into a lake that immediately dispatches concentric outreaching circles.

Eventually the little outgoing waves reverse course and return to the center. What you give out will come back to you.

Make sure all of your interactions come from a place of love, caring, understanding, and compassion. Isn't that what you want back? Study and practice the responses that connect people, create positive energy, and build trust.

CHAPTER 18 | RECOGNIZE YOUR RESOURCES

*S*ometimes you might bemoan the fact that you don't have many resources. Even if you don't have the financial authority to write big checks, give incentives or provide manpower, don't jump to the conclusion that you have nothing to offer. Money and manpower are powerful resources, but not the only bargaining chips with value. Recognize the practical resources that are within your reach.

1. Bright Ideas

2. Helping Hands

3. Kind Words

4. Bits and Pieces

5. Passion and Purpose

1. BRIGHT IDEAS

Most likely, you stay updated in your profession or industry by perusing trade journals, attending conferences, reading books, and keeping abreast of the competition. You also stay current on other topics and activities that are meaningful to you. Whether it's football, yoga, motorcycles, or quilting that piques your interest, you have knowledge or skills in your leisure time pursuits. And if you are involved in community organizations, a church, or your children's school and activities, you are close to the action and in touch with community concerns.

These three areas of knowledge and expertise: occupation, leisure, and community concerns are your fuel for bright ideas. Your ideas can be useful to others. If you see a need for information that you have, by all means share it. Give a tip, journal article, web site, idea, strategy, bargain, or trend. If you see a need for a skill you understand, share that skill. Explain how to write a grant, use a new computer program, fix the blinds, change the oil, or improve a golf swing. Look for opportunities. Use your intuition to sense whether it is appropriate to share your knowledge and expertise. Be humble. Share your bright ideas in the spirit of good will.

2. HELPING HANDS

"My dad always taught me these words: care and share. That's why we put on clinics. The only thing I can do is try to give back."

-Tiger Woods

Sometimes people ask why there is poverty, violence, homelessness, and injustice in the world. The answer is simple: people allow it. These situations happen if we ignore the issues and pass the troubles off as someone else's problem or fault. The great humanitarian Mother Teresa said: *There is a light in this world, a healing spirit more powerful than any darkness we may encounter....Then suddenly the spirit will emerge through the lives of ordinary people who hear a call and answer in extraordinary ways.* I believe the "healing spirit" is the force that

91

moves people to step out of their comfort zones and help other people, protect the environment, or champion causes like social justice and world peace.

You can reach out and use your helping hands to make another person's life better or to make the world better. It can be a simple task like helping an elderly neighbor take in the groceries or picking up littered trash along your street. Or you can volunteer to give assistance to one of many charitable and worthy causes. You can join with your colleagues at work, church or family to help in community efforts to feed the hungry, give shelter to the homeless, provide clothing, visit the sick or elderly, or clean up the environment and truly make a difference.

From time to time, everyone struggles with a work or family situation that overloads them with responsibilities, challenges, and pressures. Offering a helping hand to another person in a time of need can be greatly appreciated.

3. KIND WORDS

Kind words or bitter words; affirming or critical; accepting or rejecting; requesting or demanding—the words you use and the tone of your voice can build influence or drive wedges. Witnessing others using hurtful words is distressing. To see a parent belittling a child, an employer deriding a subordinate, or a person ridiculing a friend can be upsetting. People are receptive to positive words. Thoughtful expressions of guidance, appreciation, gratitude, or affirmation can convey the sense that you care about the person and notice their efforts. You can even express frustration and disappointment with kind words to make your point without being hurtful. You've heard the saying: *You catch more flies with honey.* Kind words can be used to:

- Make a request.

- Thank a person for assistance.

- Give guidance on your expectations.

- Express appreciation.

- Offer encouragement to do better or try again.

- Give directions for a behavior change.

- Compliment a skill or effort.

- Give feedback on performance.

- Recognize accomplishments.

- Stick up for another.

- Say good things about a person to others.

Affirming words are far more likely to motivate someone to be cooperative. A person might forget the purpose or content of your words, but they will never forget how you made them feel.

What holds you back from choosing kind words and a kind tone of voice? Will Rogers answers that: *There ain't nothing but one thing wrong with every one of us, and that's selfishness.* Get past your ego and give kind words to others. The benefit to you is a better relationship and increased influence.

4. BITS AND PIECES

Tangible items are goods that can be given or exchanged like money, supplies, or equipment. Maybe you don't have access to big tangible items, but you have bits and pieces. Giving a birthday card, a meaningful book, a cup of coffee or a chocolate chip cookie at just the right time can be a wonderful pick-me-up and an expression of caring.

My mother is the queen of bits and pieces. At any given time, she can pull out just the needed thing from her purse! A safety pin, band-aid, hand lotion, antiseptic cream, bug spray, needle and thread, scissors, flashlight, breath mints, tissue, candy, gum, pencil, paper, snacks, stamp, bottle of water...you need it, Mom probably has it handy. I don't know how she does it. I think her purse is magical.

Don't you know people at work like that? They have a well-stocked bottom desk drawer, just in case somebody needs something. Some might even have balloons, birthday candles, gag gifts, toys, a kazoo and a whoopee cushion for impromptu fun.

Be on the lookout for opportunities to provide bits and pieces as needed. You might save the day for someone.

5. PASSION AND PURPOSE

Take a minute to reflect on the following directives, or jot down your responses in the space provided.

1. Identify three things that you are enthusiastic or passionate about:

_____

_____

_____

2. Name a charity that you believe in and support with your time and/or money:

_____

_____

_____

3. Designate three character traits that you most want to be known for:

_____

_____

_____

4. Specify three things that mean pure fun for you:

_____

_____

_____

Your responses give insights into your passion and purpose in life. Your mission in life is to discover your passion and find your talents, and then give them back to the world in service. Passion and purpose. These are probably the most overlooked resources you have. Passion and purpose are the ability to inspire and motivate *others* to achieve great things. Your co-workers need your passion and purpose to fuel their own commitment. Your family members need your inspiration and vision to find their own path. Your children need your sense of fun and play to learn how to enjoy life. Your clients or customers want to work with someone who is ethical and believes that doing the right thing is not an option, it is a must. Your neighbors, church, and community are energized by your connection to social justice and environmental responsibility. These are things that you can give them every day by understanding your own passion and purpose. Robert Louis Stevenson said: *The best things are nearest: breath in your nostrils, light in your eyes, flowers at your feet, duties at your hand, the path of God just before you. Then do not grasp at the stars, but do life's plain, common work as it comes, certain that daily duties and daily bread are the sweetest things of life.*

Recognize your resources. Be more consciously aware of the valuable assets at your command, and be ready to use your resources for the common good....and for greater influence.

CHAPTER 19 | TRADE, SWAP, AND BARTER

*W*hat I didn't know about him beforehand: he had a tenacity for order; was detail-oriented; wanted to have some "think time" before making a decision; was visual and needed to see things on paper; was non-demonstrative and stoic so I couldn't read his face.

What I didn't realize about myself beforehand: I'm a big picture thinker; am energized by the final results first and work out the details as I go; like to talk through things; am emotional.

He was my boss, the assistant superintendent in the school district and in charge of me, the Wellness and Student Assistance Coordinator. All of my program ideas, initiatives, and grant proposals had to be approved by him before planning and implementation.

This is what I was doing: making an appointment to see him, pitching my idea, and bouncing it around by talking about possibilities. And this is what I was getting: He said: "Cathy put your proposal in writing and give me some time to think about it before you talk to me again." FRUSTRATION! It took me a while to figure this out:

-He was THINK ABOUT IT...I was GET IT DONE;

-He was ON PAPER...I was LET'S TALK;

-He was LOGIC...I was EMOTION.

For this exchange to work, it was critical to my busy and detail-oriented boss to get what he wanted, a proposal in writing with all the details flushed out before any discussion. Initially I was resistant. "Why doesn't he just listen to me? It would be so much faster," I lamented.

One day it hit me like a ton of bricks! Geeez! *I have to give him what he wants before I can get what I want. I have to write a proposal!* That is something I could do. It was a resource I was not using. I just had to pull out that resource, brush up on it, and just do it.

Here's what the new and improved exchange looked like: he got the summary, the key ideas, and the benefits in a brief written proposal to read and digest before my meeting with him. Here's what I got: the green light! Maybe a few questions or suggestions, but I almost always got the "go for it Cathy" green light. As an added benefit, I also obtained clarity on what I wanted by formulating the proposal, seeing the holes, and filling the gaps through the writing process. And when he had the facts, he could appreciate my enthusiasm. Now it was a win/win situation.

In my personal experience (and I bet many of you will probably agree that you've done this too) I would get so caught up with my own concerns that I didn't pay attention to what was important to the person I wanted to influence. If there was resistance, I saw it as a battle or tug of war. I didn't know how to trade, swap, or barter my resources for a mutually satisfying exchange.

I changed my thinking in order to see my boss as my ally. I made the realization that we had the same mission, staff/student wellness and achievement. We were allies, not combatants. I realized that our exchanges should get the tasks done and strengthen the relationship. Donald Trump once said: *Tasks are easy, people can be difficult.* The difficulty lay in paying attention to the other person instead of focusing on my needs or feelings. I started paying attention to what my boss said about his family, hobbies, and interests. I gained insight into his job duties, responsibilities, and pressures. I observed how he interacted with other people. I particularly listened to what he requested of me. With that information, I did see him as an ally and developed a clear understanding of what he needed from me for a collaborative work alliance. He turned out to be my best boss ever......well, until now. I have a terrific boss now who understands me in every way. I am a self-employed speaker/writer, so I'm the boss of me!

You gain influence by learning how to trade, swap, or barter your resources. Learn and practice the following steps:

1. Assess the situation and understand your stake and your needs.

2. See the other person as an ally who shares a goal with you.

3. Determine what resources your ally might want or need.

4. Clarify how you should interact with the person you want to influence by observing his/her behavioral style and asking good questions.

5. Make the exchange by giving your ally the resource he wants in the way he can best receive it.

In their book *Influence Without Authority*, Allan R. Cohen and David L Bradford say: *We have discovered that it is the process of give and take that governs influence. Making exchanges is the way to gain influence; and that process leads to cooperation rather than retaliation or refusal to engage.* Give other people what they want first and, as all great thinkers have told us, you'll get everything in life that you want. Have faith and optimism in your ability to trade, swap, and barter your resources to increase your influence.

CHAPTER 20 | FIGHT RIGHT

onflicts happen. At work, you might think that in order to keep the job and survive office politics, you must sidestep conflict or avoid disclosure of opinions and feelings. Or you might succumb to gender roles, bigger egos, or the pecking order. Conflict is inevitable and fighting is necessary. Does this statement clash with your expectations for harmony and safety? You have to fight, but in the RIGHT manner. Maybe you have trouble with those two words "fight" and "right" being put together?

The verb "to fight" means "to struggle against in any manner." The critical words "in any manner" signify that there is a wrong way and a right way to fight. Synonyms for the noun "fight" are confrontation, conflict, contest, dispute, action, disagreement, controversy, challenge. Fights and conflicts are everyday occurrences in life because people have different opinions, ideas, and preferences on just about everything.

It is a risk to disagree with someone's viewpoint or to confront someone's negative behavior, especially if you choose the wrong or *dark side*. That happens when you let negative feelings flare and turn to hurtful behaviors, like blaming others, making excuses; bringing up the past; making threats; refusing to listen; sabotaging; avoiding the issues; or losing control with emotional, verbal or physical violence. None of these ego-driven deeds solves the problem.

There is a RIGHT manner to handling conflict that produces an agreement and keeps relationships intact. It is an efficient process with four parts:

1. Don't lose your head, USE your head.

Don't let anger or frustration trigger hurtful words or behaviors that you might regret later. Lose the anger and redirect the energy to problem solving. First, listen for understanding by opening your mind and closing your mouth. Listen to what the other person has to say about the issue. Ask questions to better understand other viewpoints. You gain an edge by putting a lid on your demanding ego and letting the other person speak first You hear their viewpoints, giving you a chance to put your own ideas in perspective before speaking. And, after they get their concerns out in the open, they will be better able to listen to you. Second, think and calmly state your feelings, needs, and concerns.

Dark side: Refusing to listen, interrupting, avoiding issues, making excuses.

2. S-t-r-e-t-c-h and generate options.

Try to see the conflict situation from all sides and points of view. Formulate it in different ways. Think of a variety of possibilities to resolve the conflict, remedy the situation, or solve the problem. Keep an open mind. Take turns and work together with the other person. Discuss the options and the consequences. Attack the problem together and not each other!

Dark side: Having ego attachment to your ideas, demanding your way, feeling reluctance in seeing the good in other's ideas, focusing on your position instead of the interests of both parties.

3. You are responsible for your behavior: for what you say and do.

Enlist your best character. Be respectful. Be patient. Be persistent. Be compassionate. Be honest. Be open-minded. Be tactful. Be nice. Your character determines how you behave and perform in tough situations. You are always responsible for what you say and do, so self-govern your behavior. With a little discipline, you can align your behavior with character and act in ways that will later make you proud instead of regretful.

Dark side: Losing control, being hurtful, saying or doing inappropriate things.

4. Bring closure.

Like everything else in life, there is no one right answer here. You might be able to choose a mutually acceptable solution (win/win), clarify what you both will do or will not do as a result, agree to think it over and talk about it later, or agree to seek assistance from others. Or, you might even agree to disagree, or agree to drop it and to get over it!

Dark side: Bailing out, giving in, giving up.

It is a risk to confront an opposing viewpoint, to listen with an open mind, to be assertive, to negotiate alternatives, or to admit that you're wrong and say "I'm sorry." Take the risk to fight RIGHT. These tactics will support and validate a cooperative and harmonious work or home climate. The process and outcomes of your efforts will build more trusting relationships and maintain your influence.

CHAPTER 21 | REACH OUT

*B*elow our house runs the Sandbranch Creek. A few years ago a massive Sycamore tree that sat on the far bank of the creek was uprooted by high waters and wind. It fell over the creek and formed a bridge about fifteen feet above the water. The trunk of the tree had a very large circumference and the length completely spanned the wide creek from bank to bank. My husband cut off most of the limbs and moved them out of the way, making a natural bridge over the creek.

On a crisp November day, two of my little nephews were visiting and we went for a nature walk down by the creek. They wanted to cross the tree trunk bridge. Being a bit afraid of heights, I stayed on the bank watching them. Five-year-old Zac had no fear and bravely walked across the tree trunk, followed by my husband Grundy and then eight-year-old Jacob. When Zac neared the end of the solid trunk and reached the roots of the fallen tree, my husband told him to stop because there is no good, solid way to reach the far bank. But Zac kept right on going.

It happened so quickly! In a flash he had fallen through the roots. Amazingly, he had the agility to grab onto a root with both hands. There he was, hanging on, dangling about twelve feet above the cold creek water.

"Hang on Zachary! Be strong!" I frantically shouted. "Good job for grabbing that root!"

Grundy and Jacob quickly made their way to last solid part of the tree. My husband carefully lay down over the trunk on his tummy and stretched down for little Zachary. But he couldn't quite reach him. He had to lean farther down than his balance would allow. I saw Grundy and Jacob quickly discuss their options. Then Jacob carefully positioned his body over Grundy's legs, which were hanging off the other side of the tree trunk!

"Jake, hold on tight," I pleaded, believing that two of my sister's children who were in my care, were now in danger. Grundy slid downward a bit farther, extending with all his might. Jacob, a child diagnosed with ADHD, was remaining perfectly still and focused in his dangerous position.

"Zachary, look up and see Uncle Grundy's hand, "I instructed. "Zac, you have to grab his hand."

Suddenly, Grundy's hand held Zachary's hand. It looked like an acrobatic circus act. Grundy was hanging upside down from the tree trunk, Jacob was precariously lying over the back of Grundy's knees, and Zac was suspended over the creek dangling from a one-hand hold. I feared that any second all three would tumble into the creek, one on top of the other.

I kept up the steady stream of positive cheering from the sidelines. "Good job, Jacob. Keep hold of Grundy. Way to go Grundy, you've got him. Zac, hold on tight." Inch by inch, with amazing strength and balance, my husband was able to pull Zachary back up onto the tree trunk without knocking Jacob off either. All three of them sat there for a bit, kind of knotted around each other in a group hug, enjoying the adrenaline rush of the rescue. Then I heard my husband (the retired school principal who still uses teachable moments) gently explain why he had asked Zac to stop when he got to the roots and showed the boys that the roots were flimsy and dangerous to walk on.

"Zac, you have to learn to be safe," Grundy said softly. "I don't want anything to happen to you. You're my little peanut."

Five-year-old Zachary looked up into my husband's eyes and said, "Uncle Grundy, you're my big peanut!"

> *"In the time we have it is surely our duty to do all the good we can to all the people we can in all the ways we can."*
>
> *-William Barclay*

How many people do you know just hanging on by a thread? How many distressed, over-worked, under-appreciated or at-their-wits-end people have you seen on the edge? Think about your "big peanut" moments. When you have reached out to assist another person with your physical muscles, helping hand, on-the-edge risk taking effort on their behalf, or cheering support from the sidelines—these efforts make a difference.

There are friends, co-workers, neighbors, and family members that you were meant to reach, to bless, to change, to assist and to influence. Reach out to them.

CHAPTER 22 | SHAPE YOUR SAFETY NET

I wondered what my Aunt Bernie and Uncle Ed were doing as they moved three picnic tables together end-to-end at the annual Holmes Family Reunion. We had just finished eating; family members were socializing and re-connecting; children were moving out of the shelter house to begin spirited games. My uncle unraveled a large cylinder of butcher paper and my aunt taped it on the connecting tables.

It was the genealogy diagram of my (deceased) maternal grandparents, their seven children, thirty-seven grandchildren, numerous great grandchildren, and now a dozen or more great-great grandchildren. It was powerful to see the expanse of my extended family in connecting lines and rows. My grandmother, a true matriarch, had lived 105 years and had woven personal strong ties with most of us on the chart. She was the glue that held a large family together. She taught us the power of community, encouragement, and loving support.

It reminded me how important it is to have others who care about my growth and are willing to give me en-couragement and appropriate feedback. It doesn't matter if they are family, friends, neighbors, or co-workers. It doesn't matter if that support is within formal or informal guide-lines. Human beings are vulnerable and need advocates, coaches, cheerleaders, and friends to nurture us. We need community.

Once a month, I regularly meet with a mastermind group. We are business owners who are like-minded, have similar energy, and share the same profession. The purpose of our meetings is to support each other in our career growth as speakers and writers. We have developed objectives, formats, and rituals. We compliment and supplement each other. We brainstorm, question, challenge, critique, and create. These meetings provide us a safety net for the risky business of creating and presenting new ideas. They are an important source of giving/receiving as well as a boost for continued growth.

> *"It is one of the most beautiful compensations of this life that no man can sincerely try to help another without helping himself."*
>
> -Ralph Waldo Emerson

Informally, and always on call, I have my primary community. I rely on my family and a couple of close friends for continuous love, caring, companionship, and support. Thank goodness for my sister Nancy, who is my best friend. After living with three boisterous younger brothers for a few years, I was overjoyed to have a sister! The kinship of my primary community adds value and reassurance to my life. It makes me stronger and it makes them stronger. I know that clergy and professional service providers are there if I need them. Just as the Beatles sang: *I get by with a little help from my friends.....*

Do you have a safety net? Being part of a community allows you to participate in collective energy, hope, and healing. In the security of your safety net, you can practice mutually rewarding exchanges and build your influence. You will be more courageous about taking risks if you have needed support. Round up your advocates and shape your safety net.

CHAPTER 23 | REACH NEW HEIGHTS

*D*o you think Peter Drucker (Ch. 13) was right in predicting that social capital will drive the future? We are seeing dramatic forces of environmental disasters, ideology conflicts, international warfare, and economic instability across the globe. The effects of these forces permeate businesses, schools, churches, neighborhoods, and homes throughout the world. Now is the time for a more intense focus on social risk taking for higher level social skill performance.

"To help all created things, that is the measure of our responsibility; to be helped by all, that is the measure of our hope."

-*Gerald Vann*

Influence is your power to produce positive effects on the actions or thoughts of other people. In your circle of influence, which relationships need your attention? How can you expand your social capital? What social skills do you need to practice with more diligence? What outcomes do you expect from improving your ability to make beneficial exchanges with others? What effect can your improved social skill performance have on the quality of life in your home, your neighborhood, your community and your workplace?

Sometimes all you need is a little push to get you pumping and gliding on your own. Get along with other people. The following is a quick reminder of the nine incentives in this section to get you back in the swing of INFLUENCE:

- **Size Up Your Alliances**: Think of the other person as your ally.

- **Start Talking**: Improve your questioning savvy.

- **Look, Listen and Learn**: Understand and adapt to behavioral styles.

- **Build Trust**: Connect to people with caring actions, not selfish actions.

- **Recognize Your Resources**: Know what you have to give and be generous with your resources.

- **Trade, Swap, and Barter**: Make exchanges by giving an ally the resource she wants in the way she can best receive it.

- **Fight RIGHT**: Handle conflict and negotiation in the right manner.

- **Reach Out**: Take the risk to give resources when they are most needed.

- **Shape Your Safety Net**: Identify your advocates and nurture your networks.

Incorporating these habits into your social skill performance can help you reach new heights in INFLUENCE... Risk it!

PART III:

immediacy

Get Healthy

CHAPTER 24 | PHYSICAL RISK

The sun was shining, the air was icy cold, and fresh snow covered the tundra. Dozens of spirited huskies raced around the poles on which they were tethered when they saw her pull the sled from the barn. We helped her choose the team and harness each of the eager dogs. Finally, we were snuggled in the sled and flying across the snow on a great adventure: dog sledding in Alaska! Lorraine Temple, the seasoned dog sled musher, dog trainer, and owner of the Homer-based Outback Kachemak Dog Sled Tours, let my husband and me each have a turn at standing on the runners behind the sled while we whizzed past snow-covered pine trees. What a feeling! *Call of the wild.*

On-the-edge dangerous physical performance has never been more popular than it is now. Television, movies, and advertising— all promote the exhilarating world of physical challenge and extreme sport. Physical adventures can cut you loose from the normal routine and infuse a welcome rush of adrenaline. The power you feel after skiing down a mountain, gliding through the air under a parasail, maneuvering the rapids in a kayak—anything that physically stretches your abilities makes you feel better about yourself gives you a thrill and a sense of accomplishment.

But the *important* physical actions are what you put into your body, how you care for your body, and what you do with your body on a daily basis. Immediacy is the operative word. That means right now, with conscious intention, and without delay. Maintaining your body's health, fitness, strength, and energy is a daily challenge.

Sigmund Freud said that everything a person does springs from two motives: The desire to be great, or the sex drive. Ah, the sex drive.

Being sexy is a big deal. Is sex appeal a look, an impression or a state of mind? Advertisers try to fool us into believing that sex appeal can be created by the brand and price tag of the clothes you wear, the car you drive or the jewels that adorn your body. But that's *affluence* appeal or *attention* appeal—the *look at me and see how much I spent* allure. That is not sex appeal.

When you step out of the car, out of the clothes and adornments, the only thing that makes you sexy is your body and your feelings about your own body. A healthy body that is cared for, fit, and flexible is physically attractive and exudes the inner confidence and strength that comes from being comfortable in your own skin. The physical actions that matter are the choices you make about the food you put into your system, how you hydrate your body, the amount of sleep you get, the type and length of your exercise/fitness routine, and how you relax.

> *"I am convinced that life in a physical body is meant to be an ecstatic experience."*
>
> *-Shakti Gawain*

Your body: you wash, shampoo, shower, shave, brush, dress, adorn, and look at it every day. You spend money and time on the external looks. But are you doing the right things for its internal maintenance?

The upcoming five chapters will provide practical strategies for improving your health, well-being, and quality of life. Get healthy. Ingrain these habits–with immediacy!

CHAPTER 25 | BANISH DUMB HEALTH RISKS

*L*et's start with the dumb health risks. Many people succumb to the addictive lure of tobacco, alcohol, and other drugs. These behaviors are easy to do, easy to obtain, promoted by advertising, and modeled by stars in movies and television. These behaviors seem almost harmless and acceptable. But what are the risks to your body? Here's a reminder:

- **Tobacco:** Besides impairing your breathing, putting a rasp in your voice, making your clothes, hair and hands stink, and causing wrinkles in your skin, the health risks of tobacco use are emphysema, chronic lung disease, cancer, stroke, and heart disease. Nicotine is a powerfully addictive stimulant. Once you start, it's hard to quit.

- **Alcohol:** Moderate drinking of alcoholic beverages is not detrimental to most people. But heavy use of alcohol decreases your ability to think and function properly. It impairs your ability to drive or operate equipment because it interferes with concentration, slows down reflexes, and reduces coordination. The health risks are cirrhosis of the liver, sexual dysfunction, and fetal alcohol syndrome if a woman drinks heavily while she is pregnant. Large doses of alcohol can induce vomiting, unconsciousness, coma, and even death. There is the risk of drinking/driving and automobile crashes.

- **Drugs:** Medicines are for people who need them as prescribed by a doctor. Illegal drug use or misuse of legal drugs can do serious damage to the body. Getting high on alcohol or other drugs can be the triggering factor for risky social behaviors like violence, crime, unprotected sex, and abuse.

- **Food:** Overeating, especially food with too much fat or sugar and processed foods, can lead to obesity, heart disease, diabetes, and high cholesterol.

The big question is: Why do smart people indulge in risky behaviors that could diminish their efficiency and cause health problems? I think we've been duped! Advertising, popular culture, and social conditioning try to lead us into believing that food, tobacco, alcohol, and other drugs can help us to avert stress, deal with difficult situations, and soothe emotional pain. So some people use them to self-medicate. But at what cost to the body?

Before you make any judgments about yourself or anyone else for that matter, remember that everyone has challenges, stress, emotional pain and difficult situations. Food, tobacco, alcohol, or other drugs do nothing to resolve these circumstances. They're crutches. They're temporary fixes. And if abused, over-used, or misused, they can do damage to the body.

Back in the devastating decade of my twenties when I had many unfortunate situations (my dad's death, three miscarriages, house that burned down, and divorce), I gained weight, faced depression, and believed the advertising ploy.

I was definitely using food and alcohol to self-medicate. I told myself that I deserved these pleasures because I had such rotten luck. But it wasn't until I faced the deteriorating state of my physical and emotional health that I realized I was on the wrong track. I'd been duped. I had bought into the misconception that food and alcohol would help ease my problems. *Wrong.*

The only way through my problems was to take the risk to deal with them and not put my body in jeopardy. On the one hand, I had to deal with my problems on an intellectual and emotional level. On the other hand, I had to love my body and take better care of it. I got back on track with counseling, diet and exercise management, and lots of support from my family and friends.

"If anything is sacred, the human body is sacred."

-*Walt Whitman*

You must face your own challenges and difficulties. Wherever you are in your life's journey right now, remember that **you** make the choices. You can develop better health habits to reshape your body and how you feel about your body. Being healthy, fit, flexible, and strong causes you to look good and to feel good about your physical asset—your body.

CHAPTER 26 | KNOW YOUR NUTRIENTS

*F*ood, glorious food. It is absolutely necessary for survival and one of the real pleasures of life. I like everything about food—planning meals, perusing cook books, trying new recipes, shopping for groceries, gardening, cooking the cuisine, and savoring the smell and taste of good food. I don't like the clean up, though. Once the eating part is over, I'm done with it. So I made a deal with my husband years ago: I cook; he cleans up. He likes my cooking, so it works for us. Whether you like to cook or not, understand what your body needs for nourishment and make the right choices about what you put into your mouth— no matter who prepares it.

The nutrients in food sustain every system, function, and cell of your body. You were probably exposed to this information in a health class or science class somewhere back around middle school. But did you really learn it? Are those facts ingrained into your psyche and eating habits? Do you know your nutrients?

The CBS show *The Late Show with David Letterman* occasionally has audience participation games entitled: "Know Your....Something-Or-Other" like "Know Your Current Events," "Know Your Cuts of Meat," or "Know Your Political Figures." In that vein, this chapter is called "Know Your Nutrients."

Know Your Nutrients
Food serves the body in three ways:

1. As energy (carbohydrates and fat) to fuel your body's external movements like walking or climbing the stairs and internal actions like your heart pumping or your kidneys functioning.

2. As building blocks (protein and most minerals) to grow, maintain, and renew body parts. Every cell in your body is replaced on a continual basis.

3. As catalysts (vitamins and some minerals) to jump-start the chemical reactions needed change food into energy and into cell replacement.

The nutrients are protein, fat, carbohydrates, vitamins, and minerals. Your body needs energy, building blocks, and catalysts. But here's the bite—pun intended. If you take in too much of the energy category (carbs and fat), it is stored in your body. Think love handles, thunder thighs, or pooching belly. Your body does not store excess building blocks (protein and most minerals) or catalysts (vitamins). It uses what it needs at the moment and passes the excess. You only become aware that you lack protein, vitamins, and minerals when your body breaks down and becomes sick because of these deficiencies. Get a grip on nutrition. Provide your body with what it needs to function smoothly and stay well. And don't indulge in the super-size mentality and eat too much, especially carbs and fats, since your body will simply store those foods and pack on the pounds.

Educate yourself. Stay abreast of the latest news on nutrition research. There are many eating plans out there. What works? They all work for some people, but not for everyone! Human bodies are different, with different reactions to certain foods and eating plans. Pay attention to what certain foods do to your body, how much you need, and how eating certain foods make you feel afterwards. There is no excuse for not understanding your body and how it works. Like anything worthwhile, this takes time and effort. It takes attentiveness each time you decide to put food into your mouth.

Louise Hay says: *If it grows, eat it. If it doesn't grow, don't eat it.* That phrase has become my guiding light for my food choices. The other day, my husband and I were grocery shopping. I picked up a pineapple to put in the cart. My husband looked at the price. "For one piece of fruit, $3.95?? That's outrageous!" he exclaimed.

"The ice cream treat you had yesterday was the same price!" I retorted. "It was a snack, a treat. I paid that much for a latte this morning. This pineapple will divide into four servings. So we have two servings each of healthy fruit for the same price—a much better deal."

"Well, eating healthy is no cheap date," he complained.

"But with the high costs of health care and health insurance," I quickly replied, "we can't afford to be unhealthy."

The following is a quick reminder of what should be in your grocery cart: **things that grow.**

- **Produce:** Produces phytochemicals, the health-promoting, disease-preventing nutrient in plant foods. That is fruits and vegetables, and there are hundreds from which to choose, all chock full of vitamins and minerals. Try some new ones, find ones you like. Eat lots of fruits and veggies, preferably in their fresh natural state or frozen with no added chemicals several times a day. Studies now show that canned fruit packed in its own juices instead of heavy (high calorie) syrup has almost the same nutritional value and fiber as fresh or frozen fruit.

- **Grains**: Keep you feeling full longer and provide heart protection. The best choices are whole grains and whole grain products like oatmeal, brown rice, wheat germ, flax seed, wheat bulgur, and whole grain breads.

- **Protein sources**: Provide the amino acid leucine, which is essential for developing lean muscle mass, regulating hormones that control appetite and helping to burn calories. Lean meat, poultry, fish, eggs, beans and dairy products provide protein. Most nutrition experts recommend two servings daily, but they stress portion control. One serving is about the size of a deck of cards, not a 32-ounce steak.

- **Nuts**: The hottest in nutrition news. Researchers recommend that you eat a handful of nuts daily. Eat a variety, since all have different beneficial plant nutrients and add fiber to your diet. Just eat a handful, not the entire can.

- **Water**: The body is 60-70% water and needs to be well hydrated for the most part with pure, filtered water. Water provides your cells with life-sustaining oxygen and nutrients and flushes out toxins and waste products. Your body requires at least two quarts of water per day. An estimated 75% of

Americans are chronically dehydrated. Even a 2% drop in body water can trigger fatigue and mental dysfunction. Drink up...water, that is.

And here is a quick reminder of **things that don't grow or are not in their natural state.** Try to limit how many of these types of food are in your grocery cart:

- **Processed food:** Means anything ready-made, pre-cooked, or preserved as in just open the can, jar, box, or package and eat it or heat and serve it. In order for these foods to be ready to eat, they are made with chemicals that retard spoilage and increase shelf life. And these foods most likely have added sugar, fat, or salt to increase palatability and taste. We buy them for the convenience factor, but most have very little real nutrition. The majority of the nutrients have been processed out!

- **Sugary drinks:** Many children (and grown-ups, too) associate satisfying their thirst with a sweet drink like a can of soda, a box of juice, or a bottle of some-kind-of-*ade*. These sugary drinks can contribute to obesity. Your body has to work harder to process and eliminate the chemicals, sugar, aspartame, coloring, and phosphoric acid in soda.

Convenience is important, but HEALTH is much more important. So be a smart shopper. Read those labels and opt for nutrition, not convenience.

Busy schedules, fast-food drive-through windows, and the abundance of soda and sugary snack vending machines can result in poor eating habits.

"The secret to healthy aging is not in pharmaceuticals, surgical procedures or exotic, alchemical formulas; it is in the food we put on our plates."

-Brian Clement & Theresa Foy DiGeronimo

Absent-minded and quick decisions about food can be detrimental to your health, your emotional state, and your energy level. Make conscious choices about what you put into your body. Know what your body needs and choose your foods with awareness.

Ask your body what it needs. When you are about to make choices in a restaurant, grocery store, or standing in front of your opened refrigerator, ask your body what it needs right now. Not what it desires (because of advertising ploys), or what it wants (because of emotional pain), or what it craves (because of sugar addiction or poor food habits), but what it needs to be healthy. Don't think diet, or restriction, or "I-can't-have-that-so-I-want-it-more-than-anything" thoughts. That type of thinking only leads to rebellion. Realize that there is an abundance of healthy choices. Give yourself a moment to realize what your body needs. Then give yourself a chance to choose what is best for you.

If you are still in a quandary about what to eat, seek nutritional counseling from your doctor, a nutrition expert, on-line resources, or from the surplus of health and nutrition books on the market. There is no excuse to be misinformed about your body and what it needs to look and feel healthy. Eat healthy foods with pleasure, knowing that you are giving your body what it needs to be healthy and perform well.

CHAPTER 27 | SACK THE SLOUCH POTATO

*H*ave you ever felt tight and stiff like the Tin Man without oil? Do you have aches and pains in places you never felt before? Ever pulled a muscle when forced to move quickly, lift something heavy, or turn too sharply? Ever felt totally drained of energy like you've just run a half marathon but you haven't lifted a finger physically? Then you probably have a common affliction: NOT ENOUGH EXERCISE. Maybe you think that exercise is what causes aches, pain, and muscle soreness? Who wants that? So, back to the couch? Do you put a series of obstacles or excuses between you and a fitness routine? Do you exercise out of duty and hate every minute of it?

THE IMPRESSIVE BENEFITS OF EXERCISE

Physical benefits:	Internal benefits:	Emotional benefits:
Weight control	Cardiovascular	Natural highs
Body contouring	Circulatory	Stress reliever
Flexibility and strength	Digestive	Mood lifter
Energy boost	Respiratory	Self-esteem enhancer
Sexy appearance	Immune	Relaxation response

Consider the benefits. Exercising enhances your appearance and creates an aesthetic feeling. It's good for your physical and mental health. The most recent Federal Guide-lines tell us to engage in regular physical activity and reduce sedentary activities to promote health, psychological well-being, and a healthy body weight. Ideally, you need 30 minutes of moderate intensity physical activity at least 5 times a week for optimal fitness. If that seems inappropriate for your busy schedule, break it down to 10 or 15 minutes every day. Most experts agree that you can and should count small doses of physical exertion. Here are some frequently given examples that you can start to do immediately:

- Forego the elevator and take the stairs a few times a day.

- Give yourself a 5-minute break and do some stretching exercises.

- Park at the far end of a parking lot and walk briskly to your destination.

- Get on the floor and do leg lifts or sit-ups as you watch the evening news.

Each of the three types of physical exertion has terrific physical, internal, and emotional benefits. Aerobic exercise increases your heart rate (cycling, walking, or tennis). Stretching exercise increases flexibility to your joints and muscles (yoga or dancer's stretches). Resistance exercise tones and builds your muscle mass (lifting weights or using resistance bands or machines). If you hate one, try something else. Find one you like. Match it to your behavioral style. Take this quick quiz to find a match.

EITHER.....OR

1. Choose one:

_____I am an **extrovert** *(I get energy from other people)*
...OR.....

_____I am an **introvert** *(I get energy from within myself and need time alone)*

2. Choose one:

_____**I prefer a fast, lively pace**   ...OR...
_____**I prefer a slower,** more deliberate pace

3. Choose one:

_____I like structure/organization   ...OR...
_____I am a free-spirit

4. Choose one:

_____I prefer being indoors   ...OR...
_____I prefer outdoors

If you are an extrovert who gains energy from other people, try a group physical activity like playing on a softball team, biking with friends, or taking a group exercise class at a gym or fitness center. If you're an introvert who gains energy from self and needs time alone, take solitary walks, buy free weights or an exercise video and work out in your own home.

If you prefer a fast and lively pace, perhaps a spinning class, aerobics, or tennis would match your tempo. But if slower, more deliberate timing is to your liking, maybe you'd be happier with the pace of yoga, tai chi, or leisurely swimming laps.

If you like structure and organization, join a gym/fitness center and get one of their experts to craft an exercise routine for you or hire a personal trainer to coach you through a planned series of exercise. But if the term "free spirit" defines your style, let your spirit of adventure and whimsy guide you to jump on a trampoline one day, run through the park another day, and dance wildly at a club another day.

Do you prefer to be indoors where it is climate-controlled, insect-free, and not ruled by weather conditions? Then by all means, choose indoor fitness activities. But if you love trees, sunshine, and wind in your face, then get outdoors to exercise. There is no one "right" way to exercise. It depends on individual likes, preferences, and habits. There are so many possibilities.

You've heard the philosophy: "No pain...is no pain!" If you experience any pain during exercise, *stop*. Adjust the activity to your needs or try another form of physical activity. Of course if you have high blood pressure, have had recent surgery, experience back or knee pain or haven't been physically active for a long time, see your doctor for advice on how to safely incorporate exercise into your daily routine.

In June of 2004, I learned the hard way never to be too cocky or take my health and fitness for granted either. I was volunteering for a charity event held at the Kansas Speedway. The day before the event, my husband, my nephew and I were helping set up the silent auction in one of the infield garages and the banquet in another garage. There was a concrete parking lot in between the two garages. We had jogged across the parking lot two or three times because it was lightly raining. Then we had to go back to the other garage again. This time, my nephew Zachary set the challenge:

"Aunt Cathy and Uncle Grundy, I'll race you."

I love a challenge and I like to run. We took off running at full speed. Half way across the parking lot, the Achilles tendon on my right leg snapped and I went down. A few days later I had surgery and was in a cast for the next three months—which was the entire summer. Three months of being disabled and on crutches taught me to have more empathy for those who permanently endure a disabling condition. It also gave me a revived appreciation of my physical health and a renewed commitment to taking care of my body.

It is perfectly okay to gripe about exercise sometimes. It is okay to take a few days off if you're sick or on vacation occasionally. But keep in mind that exercise is a lifelong necessity and it needs to be a part of your normal daily routine. Exercise is the primary benchmark of well being. When life gets too busy or too stressful, exercise is most likely the first thing to be dropped from your routine. But if you eliminate exercise, you are eliminating a wonderful source of physical and psychological energy as well as a major means of keeping your body's 600 muscles fit, flexible, and strong.

The fact is that 95% of us will never possess the physical attributes of movie stars, models or celebrity athletes. We might never have a trophy body with enviable parts; however, the majority of us can possess a good body image. That's a realistic view of your body by keeping it healthy, fit, and strong. Sack the slouch potato. Get up and get some daily exercise. Take care of what you've got, love what you've got, and celebrate what your body can do.

Make exercise a priority.... it should be. Write exercise time down on your calendar or day planner. A new addition to your routine just takes a little planning, effort, and discipline to transform it into a new healthy habit.

CHAPTER 28 | KEEP YOUR ZZZZs

Sleep, precious sleep. Are you getting enough? How many hours of sleep do you need each night to feel great, stay awake and remain alert the next day? Do you get what you need regularly? Cutting back on sleep may seem like a good way to get a few extra hours, but it can take its toll on your productivity, safety, and health.

If you are habitually short-changing yourself of needed sleep, you put yourself at risk for agitation, fatigue, loss of focus, and impaired thinking speed. Sleep deprivation can increase the possibility of auto crashes and on-the-job accidents. National Highway Traffic Safety reports that sleepy drivers are involved in 100,000 automobile crashes which result in more than 40,000 injuries and 1,500 deaths each year. Lack of sleep creates health risks— high blood pressure, heart disease, diabetes. If that's not bad enough, lack of sleep can cause an imbalance of hormones that store and burn fat, resulting in weight gain!

Keep your ZZZZs. Sleep is healing. It is your body's renewal period. Extensive repairs, restoration, and cell replacements happen at night. Your body completely renews itself. Sometimes it's hard to go from "full speed ahead" to "go to sleep." A bedtime routine can help you transition from a busy state to a relaxed state. Try deep breathing, visualization, inspirational reading, taking a warm bath, listening to calm, restful music, or light stretching exercises.

A peaceful frame of mind enhances your sleep time. Watching disturbing TV news, violent or scary movies, or reading something that upsets you before you go to bed can agitate your mental state. *Kiss and make up before going to bed* is also good counsel. I'm amused by Phyllis Diller's advice: *Never go to bed mad. Stay up and fight!* Try to resolve issues or put an issue on hold until the next day in a loving way. Much clearing work is done in the dream state so you don't want to take negative thoughts or feelings into your sleep.

If you experience recurring or chronic problems with insomnia, see a doctor. You might have a condition (sleep apnea, thyroid irregularities, depression) or a contributing health problem that can be diagnosed and treated.

A good night's sleep on a regular basis is a good investment. Take the risk to invest your time wisely. Keep your ZZZZs. The right amount of sleep will keep you refreshed, alert, and ready for peak performance.

CHAPTER 29 | LET EVERYTHING GO

$\mathcal{T}$hink about the last time you had the opportunity to let everything go, give your brain a rest, put your cares aside, truly relax, and be carefree even if only for a few minutes. Maybe you were doing something very simple and enjoyable like floating in a swimming pool, petting an animal or just swinging on the porch swing. You need little shots of this letting-everything-go state regularly.

Robert Benson coined the phrase "relaxation response" in the 70s. Look at the following rewards of achieving this state of relaxation:

- Your heart slows down.

- Your blood pressure drops.

- Your muscles relax.

- Your breathing slows.

- Your digestive process improves.

- Your brain waves go into a mode of peace and calm.

Sounds like a little bit of heaven, doesn't it? You might think that the wonderful benefits of the relaxation response can only be achieved through long meditative sessions. The reason that meditation is called a "practice" is that it takes practice. Meditation is the state of being which brings stillness to body and mind. It is an exercise that deeply relaxes the physical body and keeps the mind completely blank with no thoughts. This state may be maintained for a few minutes or a few hours, depending upon your skill.

AROMATHERAPY

Aromatherapy is one of the fastest-growing fields in alternative medicine. This holistic treatment of caring for the body involves using pleasant-smelling botanical oils such as rose, lemon, lavender, and peppermint. These oils can be added to a bath or massaged into the skin; inhaled directly or diffused into an entire room. Aromatherapy is used to relieve pain, care for the skin, alleviate tension or fatigue, and invigorate the entire body. Essential oils can affect the mood, alleviate fatigue, reduce anxiety, and promote relaxation. Some of the claims of the benefits of aromatherapy are:

- *cinnamon fights colds and flu;*

- *lavender soothes burns and heals wounds;*

- *peppermint is a stimulant and can get rid of headaches, fever and chills;*

- *rosemary helps improve memory; rose oil is an antidepressant and helps cope with grief.*

You can also reap the rewards of the letting-everything-go state by understanding how to use your assets in mindfulness. Mindfulness means giving your undivided attention to something. Your assets for achieving the relaxation state in mindfulness are... your senses. You can practice by letting everything go for a few minutes and giving your attention to something through your senses:

1. **Sight:** Look at or imagine things that are visually beautiful to you like a crimson leafed maple tree in the fall, a lovely fire in the fireplace, your baby peacefully sleeping, or a sunset over the ocean.

1. **Sounds:** Delight in sounds that soothe your soul like wonderful music, birds chirping in the woods, or rain drops on the roof.

2. **Smells:** Experts in aromatherapy propose that scents can affect mood and promote a sense of well-being. Enjoy pleasing smells like sniffing the freshness of clean sheets, brewing cinnamon tea or picking a basil leaf off the plant, rubbing it between your fingers and inhaling the scent.

3. **Touch:** Luxuriate in pleasant, tactile sensations like petting an animal, kneading bread dough, relaxing in a bubbling hot tub, or treating yourself to a massage.

4. **Taste:** Be gratified by the delectable taste of your favorite foods like a perfectly grilled and seasoned salmon filet, a ripe, just-picked-from-the-tree, juices-running-down-your-chin peach, or a decadent a hot fudge sundae.

Even though you have an active and busy life, you can seek small doses of serenity and calm. The ability to let everything go and focus on a sensory pleasure can help you achieve the relaxation response. The longer you can hold your concentration, the more beneficial it will be.

When relieved of pressure, your mind has time to rearrange itself, a chance to create positive energy, and space to feel inner peace. After achieving the relaxation response, you will emerge with a clearer mind, sharper thoughts, and a refreshed body.

CHAPTER 30 | REACH NEW HEIGHTS

What are your goals for immediacy? Good health and well being? Fitness and toned body? Longevity and quality of life? Sex appeal? Understand how you will achieve your goals. Refuse to let bad habits like laziness, convenience-over-health, or so-

"Keeping your body healthy is an expression of gratitude to the whole cosmos—the trees, the clouds, everything."

-Thich Naht Hanh

cial conditioning hinder your physical performance. The desire to be healthy can call forth the best in you.

Parts of the body sometimes malfunction. Accidents occur. Illness does happen. Get medical attention when you need it. Lovingly forgive your body for breakdowns and continue to give it what it needs to regain health and strength. Just thinking "I hope nothing goes wrong" is not good enough. Hope is not a basis for choice in physical risk taking. Too much is at stake. Don't whine or moan or give excuses. Start taking the right risks for your health immediately.

Get and stay healthy. Do you need a little push to get you pumping and gliding on your own? The following is a quick reminder of the five critical elements in this section to get you back in the swing of immediacy:

- **Banish Dumb Health Risks:** Consider the behaviors that put your health at risk and face your challenges.

- **Know Your Nutrients:** Make good food choices based on nutrition.

- **Sack the Slouch Potato:** Get off the couch and custom design an exercise plan to match your own behavioral style.

- **Keep Your ZZZZs:** Make it a priority to get a good night's sleep on a regular basis.

- **Let Everything Go:** Learn and practice ways to attain the relaxation response.

Bring back your natural splendor with these all-natural boosters. Get healthy. Incorporating these habits into your physical performance can help you reach new heights! **IMMEDIACY....Risk it!**

PART IV:

integrity
Get Emotionally Fit

CHAPTER 31 | EMOTIONAL RISK

It should have been a moment of glory, but it turned out to be one of the most embarrassing moments of my life. It was the first NFL Super Bowl in the

> *"There is no safety. Only varying degrees of risk."*
> -Lois McMaster Bujold

Los Angeles Coliseum, a first-time, history making event, and I was there! What a rush! I wanted to remember everything—the excitement and hoopla, thousands of noisy fans, famous Hollywood people in the audience, cameras everywhere, and all on national television—

"Hi Mom!"

I was a cheerleader for the Kansas City Chiefs with pom-poms, the big, heavy, crepe paper pom-poms of that era; not the tiny, shiny, lightweight pom-poms of this era. And I wore a high necked, long sleeved, pleated skirt, wool uniform of that era; not the tiny, shiny, lightweight outfits of this era.

I was excitedly watching the game when the Chiefs made a great play. I turned to the crowd, dropped the pom-poms on the ground, leapt into the air with a split leg, toe touch jump, landed, planted my left foot and finished with a flashy "GO CHIEFS" high kick move. Oh it was a beautiful kick--straight leg, up in the air by my head, pointed toes, one to be proud of. But my other foot, the one that was supposed to stay firmly planted on the ground, landed on the edge of a pom-pom and ....slipped! I was momentarily off balance, airborne, with legs and arms flailing to recover. I made a very ungraceful landing on my rear end on top of my pom-poms...AT THE SUPER BOWL! Embarrassment is a nasty, negative feeling.

Embarrassment ranks right up there with anger and frustration on the top of my crummy feelings list. In your past experiences, have you ever been so embarrassed by your own clumsy action or inappropriate behavior that you wanted to crawl into a hole and hide? Have you ever been so frustrated by being forced to change, adapt, or adjust--and you didn't want to or see the need for it—that you wanted to throw in the towel and quit? Ever been so angry with another person that you wanted to hurt them?

How you handle a negative emotion determines your next words and actions. Some handle it well, and some don't. Let's face it. We live in a crazy world of emotional ineptitude where people are losing control, abusing others, acting out road rage, even shooting co-workers because they can't deal with negative feelings. Safety and security are huge issues today. What does it take to be safe and secure? Video cameras in every corner? More security guards? Cell phones with 911 on speed dial?

Let me tell you. We need *emotionally stable people.* We need people who understand emotions—their expression, internalization, and how long to hold on to them. We need people who take the risk to control their state of being, self-govern their behavior, and maintain their integrity. The next ten chapters offer practical strategies for emotional risk taking. Good luck with this endeavor. I'll be cheering for you.

CHAPTER 32 | GET DOWN TO THE "REAL NITTY GRITTY"

*E*ver since I learned to read, I have always loved to read out loud. I love the sound, texture, and feel of certain words. Even as a child, I knew the power of the spoken word. At home, my mother would encourage me to read out loud to my younger siblings. She taught me how to use inflection, pauses, and expression to increase the impact of the words. She didn't realize it then (well, she probably did—my mom has always had an amazing way of knowing things ahead of time), but she was nurturing a future public speaker.

In elementary school, I always volunteered to be the speaker or the reader. And I definitely remember the first time I experienced one of my favorite words: INTEGRITY. When I came to this word, I had no idea what it meant or how to pronounce it. So, not wanting to stumble or act uncertain, I proudly pronounced it as I saw it: "intee-gritty!" with the emphasis on "gritty." Much to my chagrin, my teacher burst out laughing! My classmates didn't know the word either, so we were all curiously watching the teacher and waiting for an explanation of this funny word that made our teacher laugh.

The teacher explained that it was my pronunciation of the word that was humorous, not the word itself. She explained that the meaning of integrity was the quality or state of being complete or whole; and that a person of integrity was one of faith, honor, and virtue—the "real nitty gritty" essential parts of being a good person and doing the right thing. She cleverly connected my mispronunciation to a special insight about the meaning of the word. I quickly learned the correct way to pronounce *integrity* but every time I see the word, I chuckle and think of the "real nitty gritty."

Because of this, integrity has held a special significance for me. Is integrity important to you? Integrity is performance-based. It is about who you are in your personal and business life. It anchors your reputation, character, and ethics. It's the virtue that helps you integrate your behavior with your beliefs and values. Integrity is never a done deal or a finished product. Your life circumstances produce instant on-the-job-training. You grow in the process. Those circumstances, however, should never be allowed to control your emotional state or your behavior. Your integrity must control your state and behavior. In her book *Molecules of Emotion,* Candace Pert tells us: *Aim for emotional wholeness.* Integrity is the core principle—the real nitty gritty—of emotional wholeness.

CHAPTER 33 | RECOGNIZE THE SIGNALS

*E*motions are electromagnetic charges of energy that go zipping through your body. A negative emotion is a signal to your brain to warn you of possible threat, deficiency or insecurity. It's a signal (like a flashing light or a siren) to motivate you to protect yourself, correct an error, or make things right. Daniel Goleman, author of *Emotional Intelligence*, suggests that the quality of emotional intelligence in leaders plays a far greater role than IQ or technical skills.

You know what's weird about negative feelings? They can either hit you out of the blue like a lightning bolt—BAM!—and knock you off center. For example, you're driving along the freeway, calmly minding your own business and a speeding car suddenly cuts in front of you causing you to slam on the brakes, narrowly avoiding a crash—BAM!—lightning bolt of anger! Or a negative feeling can *s-n-e-a-k* up on you. For example, you're diligently working on a project with a deadline and you're plagued with endless interruptions (phone rings, beeper beeps, "you've got mail", people come in and demand something of you) and gradually you develop a full-blown case of overwhelming anxiety and tension!

Whether it's a sudden BAM or a sneaky intrusion, everyone experiences bad feelings and the negative state change they cause. How you handle the negative state change makes all the difference.

The root word of emotion is motion. A negative emotion shouldn't be allowed to hang around. It needs to be put in motion and moved out. Otherwise it can escalate, turn to rage, and result in hurting others with your words or actions. Or, it can be stuffed away. It remains in you and you remain unforgiving, frustrated and angry. Ralph Waldo Emerson's words are worth remembering: *For every minute you are angry, you lose sixty seconds of happiness.*

Recognize the negative emotion as a signal and move it out. Let go of negative feelings. Letting go. Why is that such a difficult thing? It reminds me of learning to water ski. The first thing you learn is that when you fall, let go of the rope or you get relentlessly dragged through the water.

Let go of negative feelings and the accompanying ego anxieties like blame, finger pointing and *why me* thoughts. Let go of what's been done in the past in order to free your mind to new possibilities. If you don't let go of negative feelings, you allow yourself to be dragged through mental anguish. Understand that a negative feeling is a signal that is alerting you to pay attention to the situation.

Recognize the signal and let go of the emotion. The person with integrity knows how to recover from the stress of a negative emotion and how to regain emotional stability.

"We need anger to define our boundaries; grief to deal with our losses; and fear to protect ourselves."

-Candace Pert

CHAPTER 34 | KEEP YOUR COOL

*Y*es, you have to *recover* from the stress of a negative emotion. The stress state happens when things are bothersome or unstable, or you are forced to change or adjust. The 1950s research by Dr. Hans Selye, the "father of stress", shows that one of the negative results of too much stress is an overdose of cortisol. Cortisol is a chemical that is released into your body when you experience the fight-or-flight response. Cortisol creates the energy to fight or run. But in work and family-related stress situations, physically fighting or running away are not viable options. It is risky to have too much cortisol in your body. Too much of it can damage your immune system; increase the risk of illness; lead to heart failure; and hamper physical, mental, and emotional performance.

How do you know if there is cortisol in your body, possibly causing damage? You most likely will experience some type of muscle tension and body aches. Cortisol puts your muscles on high alert for action, but most of the time it is inappropriate to fight or flee. Since the cortisol energy for action is not used, it manifests itself in muscle tension. Some people try to cope with stress in negative ways like smoking, drinking, or stress-induced eating, all of which have harmful effects and do nothing to help come to grips with the situation.

As if we don't have enough stress-inducing problems in our own lives, we also often become involved in other people's stress. Someone tells you about their stressful event and you can get all worked up about it, too.

Learn to positively deal with your own stress state. Some people think that stress management means you have contain negative emotions and struggle with stress-related physical symptoms all day. Then when you get home, you can go for a run, sit in the hot tub, or do some type of feel-good thing to melt away the day's stresses. That's an incorrect assumption. They are two separate things: One is dealing with the stress state when it happens, and the other is relaxation. Both are important, but separate.

Deal with the stress state at the time it happens. When situations occur that cause you to experience negative feelings and physical stress symptoms, you need a process to defuse those symptoms on the spot. Instead of going into the fight-or-flight response sending harmful cortisol into your system, you must reduce the arousal and recover your emotional stability. Keep your integrity intact by keeping your cool. The following list contains tricks to help you keep your cool:

Breathe: Deep breathing, belly breathing, yoga breathing—whatever you want to call it—just breathe slowly and deeply. Slowly fill up your belly with air, expand your lower lungs with air, then upper lungs, finally think about getting air up into your brain. Exhale slowly, repeating to yourself: "Relax, relax, relax." A good deep breath will take about 15-20 seconds. Practice it. Do it right now so you understand what it feels like.

This is a simple but powerful tool for two reasons. First, it gives a pop of circulation to every cell in your body and brings in pure, clean, healing oxygen. It sends oxygen to your brain. The brain is 2% of the body's weight, but requires 25% of the body's oxygen. An influx of oxygen opens your brain for thinking. And second, when you say that important word "relax," you give your body permission to release the physical symptoms of stress. Deep breathing is like pressing the reset button. It helps you become centered and calm.

Don't blow, re-direct the flow: A negative feeling shouldn't cause you to blow up, push your buttons and cause inappropriate behavior, or store inside and cause stress-related diseases. Put that negative emotion in motion and release it. Let it go. That is easier said than done. The trick is to respond quickly by redirecting the flow of positive feelings back into your system. You need a trigger, a slice of happy memory, a sure-fire way to infuse good feelings. My trigger is a delightful recollection of a precious moment with my granddaughter Madalyn. Her mother Susan (my daughter-in-law), Madalyn (2 ½ years old at the time), and I went to visit a friend. When we arrived, the friend had just made cookies. Turning to Maddie with a plate of cookies, she asked, "Madalyn, would you like to have a cookie?"

Of course, little Madalyn nodded her head and re-sponded quickly, "Yes!" Then the friend proposed, "Well Madalyn, what's the *magic word?*" Maddie's face lit up. She lifted her arms and exclaimed: "Ta-Da!"

Her response was so unexpected and charming. It brought immediate laughter. We were expecting her to think of manners and say "please and thank you," but her thoughts were propelled by the word *magic*! That moment in time serves me well as my special trigger. I know it brings a powerful surge of happiness. I use it any time a negative feeling has upset my state of being. My trigger helps me move out the bad feeling by the quick replacement of positive emotion.

You have a lifetime of wonderful memories (birth of a child, skiing down the black slope, child graduating, first kiss). Think about your precious moments of love, gratitude, appreciation, delight, adventure, or pure joy. Find your own trigger to jump-start a positive state change. Decide on one powerful memory right now. Have it ready to use when you need to redirect the flow.

Take control: Now that you are centered and in a positive state, you can access your problem-solving ability, interpersonal skills, and proficiency in communication. From past experience, you know those talents go AWOL when you're in a negative state. Bad feelings seem to shut down your abilities. Take just a couple of focused minutes to breathe deeply and use your trigger to redirect into a positive state to regain your abilities. Then you can take control and do the right thing. From a centered and positive state, determine what you can do to change the situation, improve the situation, or remove yourself from it.

"If you can keep your head when all about you Are losing theirs and blaming it on you. If you can trust yourself when all men doubt you And make allowance for the doubting, too."

-Rudyard Kipling

The next time you are faced with a stressful situation that makes your head spin or your blood boil, don't lose your head and do something you might regret later. Remember these tricks: Breathe, re-direct to a positive state, and take control of the situation. In this crazy world, the ability to deal with stress and keep your cool is a valuable asset. Keeping your cool allows you to keep your integrity.

35 | COP AN ATTITUDE

*A*ttitudes and moods are temporary states of mind. Attitudes have the potential to be constructive or destructive. They are produced by your thoughts, by what you think about YOU: how you look; how others perceive you; how you perform on the job; how you fare in relationships. Thoughts of blame, worry, guilt, or poor-me-ism can result in feeling bad, being in a bad mood, and having a baaaad attitude. Thoughts of satisfaction, goodwill, approval, appreciation, or gratitude can create good feelings, a good mood, and a good attitude.

Your own internal dialogue, what goes on inside your head (and I guarantee, there is a lot going on inside your head) is what creates either a positive or negative attitude or mood. Let's say you are "bammed" by a lightning bolt of anger because someone does an injustice to you. Your head might start spinning with questions like:

- Why does this always happen to me?

- Do I have to put up with this?

- What is wrong with that person?

- Why do I have to do this?

- Who's to blame?

- How can I protect my ego and hurt back?

- Why am I always so stupid?

These types of questions are easy to ask because they are "me-centered." Your EGO is talking and these questions reflect personal fear and distress. You've become offended and are in the grips of your ego.

The funny thing about your brain is that it will answer any question you pose to it. Let's take this example. In a moment of frustration, you think: "Why am I so stupid?" Your brain immediately searches and answers: *That's easy. I have a closed mind, don't learn from my mistakes, and never try anything new. Mrs. Smith gave me an F in 6th grade science so I was stupid then. Obviously I'm still stupid.* These thought ramblings cause you to become fearful, edgy and anxious. You have copped a bad attitude.

It doesn't have to be that way. Attitude is critical to your success. Attitude drives everything you do. Experts in peak performance tell us that attitude is at least 80% of success. Learn how to cop a new attitude.

CHAPTER 36 | RESTRUCTURE YOUR MENTAL INTERROGATION

In the 1960s Dr. Aaron Beck developed the system of psychotherapy called Cognitive Therapy. In this process, a therapist works with a client to overcome difficulties by changing thinking, behavior, and emotional responses. Dr. Beck's work can help all of us.

Change your thinking. That's a powerful directive. Your brain is constantly on the run—questioning, reviewing, critiquing, or second-guessing. Don't let it run rampant on a negative or destructive path. Discover how to restructure your mental interrogation. By consciously posing better questions, you can allow a more neutral or expanded view of the situation. The trick is bypassing your ego...and that's not easy. It takes effort and lots of practice. You can change your thoughts, direct the flow of positive energy back into your body and change your attitude by asking "solution-centered" questions like the following:

- How can I connect with this person?

- What is our issue?

- How can I ease this situation?

- What are my options?

- How can I best make my point?

- What am I proud of?

- What can I be thankful for?

- What can I learn from this?

- What can I do to bring peace, wholeness, healing to this situation?

Learn to observe your thought patterns. Pay attention. Troubles begin with a lousy question you put to your brain and you allow it to fester to the point of distress. When you recognize a negative stream of thinking, tell your brain to STOP. Take control and re-structure your mental interrogation.

You cannot control life's circumstances or what other people say or do. You can control what you think and therefore self-govern your behavior and attitude. Shut down your ego by immediately posing solution-centered questions. Good questions get good answers from your brain. Good answers allow you to act with integrity.

CHAPTER 37 | MAKE GRIEF AS BRIEF AS POSSIBLE

"Big Bear." That's what they called my dad at work. He was the plant supervisor for a printing company. During the summer months of my college years, I worked for my dad. I watched him manage and lead; observed his interactions at work; understood why they called him "Big Bear." He could be snarly, demanding, and on a rampage when a deadline needed to be met. Or he could be sweet and cuddly as a teddy bear, offering deserved praise, giving pats on the back, and telling jokes with his ready smile.

This experience helped me understand his reactions at home. I could see that when he was pushy and overbearing, one of us needed his strength to achieve our goals. When he was playful, loving, and protective, we needed that teddy bear warmth of security.

In the summer after my college graduation, we took our last family vacation. My dad, mom, three brothers, sister, and I went camping in the Colorado Rocky Mountains. We hiked, climbed, swam, or rode horses during the day and sang around a campfire at night. What made this vacation so bittersweet was a photograph taken of my Dad in the Garden of the Gods. He was known for "sneak attacks". Without our knowledge, he hiked up ahead of us, hid in the big rocks and waited. At just the right time, he charged out in "Big Bear" pose, growling, and scaring all of us. I snapped a picture of him--ball cap turned around backwards, standing tall, arms spread out, and hands shaped into claws, with a huge grin on his face. What just seemed crazy and fun at the moment, turned out to be a most prized photo of the essence of my dad.

Three months later, my father experienced a deadly heart attack. It was sudden and totally unexpected. We were grief-stricken. Our dad was so young and fit. He was strong as a bear. We loved him fiercely; we needed him. But now he was gone. And there was nothing anybody could do. It tore a huge hole in everyone's hearts.

One of a person's deepest fears is losing a loved one. It happens to everyone sooner or later. You get walloped by an inevitable fact of life: People die. The grieving process cycles through denial, hysteria, depression, and blame. I was unprepared for it. I held onto grief, used it as an excuse, and wielded it as a shield. After many years, I mustered the courage to seek counseling. With help, I was able to let go of the grief of losing and hold on to the happiness of loving. I wish I hadn't waited so long to get help in the healing process. My advice to anyone in throes of sorrow is to get **help**. Make grief as brief as possible and get on with living and loving.

That picture of my dad in the Garden of the Gods is old and faded, but is still a family treasure. A few years ago, my brother Gary was transferred to Colorado Springs. Another brother Jamey went to visit him in the fall. For Christmas that year, we all received a framed photograph of Gary and Jamey in the exact same spot in the Garden of the Gods, mimicking our dad in the same "Big Bear" pose, with the same big grin, thirty-something years after our last family vacation. It was a needed infusion of big bear energy—fierce action for achievement and loving spirit for encouragement. It touched our hearts and made us all remember the happiness of loving.

CHAPTER 38 | FIRE YOUR TRESPASSERS

*W*hen my grandson Mac was 4 years old, we went for a walk on our farm. As we entered the woods close to the road, Mac saw one of the yellow "No Trespassing" signs my husband had posted on a tree. At age four, he was aware of words and was learning to read.

"Grandma Cathy, what does that yellow sign say?" he asked.

"Mac, that sign says 'No Trespassing.' A trespasser is a person who enters another person's land unlawfully. The yellow sign tells people that this is private property and they should not be here without our permission."

He thought for a minute as we walked on. Then he stopped abruptly and said, "I thought we were supposed to forgive our trespasses."

Brilliant! It was another precious moment.

Can you forgive your trespasses? Those past failings can linger in your sub-conscious causing guilt, shame, and remorse. Self-forgiveness is necessary for all the mistakes and misjudgments you have made in the past. You can't take back harsh words, bursts of impatience, wrong turns, or bad choices. But you can learn the lessons of your trespasses, forgive yourself, and release the guilt that holds you back from experiencing emotional peace.

Undoubtedly, other people have made mistakes and hurt you. If you continue to hold onto the pain of being disillusioned, deceived, or dumped and harbor ill will towards those that "did unto you," you are only hurting yourself. You remain ensnared in negative thoughts and feelings, blocking your own positive energy flow.

So fire your trespassers! Donald Trump is famous for saying: "You're FIRED!" *Fire your trespassers*. Tell them to take their belongings and take a hike. Forgiving yourself and others means letting the past *be* past. It involves choosing to release resentment or guilt. Begin to replace the negative side effects of your own and other's trespasses with good deeds. Practice patience, generosity, honesty, trust, compassion and understanding that heal and fortify your emotional state. Open up the enormous power of the present to choose—again and again—thoughts, words, and actions that radiate positive energy and love.

> *"Forgiveness means giving up all hope for a better past."*
>
> -Lily Tomlin

It was a surprising, but guiding question: "Aren't we supposed to forgive our trespasses?" What a robust bit of wisdom from a four-year-old!

CHAPTER 39 | LEARN TO AFFIRM

Shakti Gawain, in her popular book *Creative Visualizations*, explains:

To affirm means to 'make firm. An affirmation is a strong, positive statement that something is already so. She gives many examples of short, simple, and effective statements that convey a strong, positive feeling. An affirmation statement simply affirms your goodness or asserts your ability to handle any situation that comes your way.

The following are some of the examples I have created that work for me in my especially difficult situations:

Cathy's Situation:	Cathy's Affirmation Statement:
I am feeling uncertain about my career direction.	My inner wisdom will guide me now.
I have been hurt and want to lash out and hurt back.	I am loving and kind.
I am in a conflict or controversy with another person.	The peace within me can transform this situation.
A person or situation causes me to feel unworthy or powerless.	I am lovable and capable.

In these types of situations, it is easy for me to be carried away by feelings of blame, guilt, and resentment. These are my pressure points or hot buttons. Take a few minutes to determine your most difficult situations and jot them down. Then create a short, positive statement that affirms your goodness or asserts your ability to handle it.

My Situation: My Affirmation:

_____   _____

_____   _____

_____   _____

_____   _____

_____   _____

_____   _____

_____   _____

Taking a few seconds to repeat an affirmation is a great way to jump-start some positive energy, transform your attitude, and refresh your mood. From a place of inner strength, your outflow— your words, actions, and body language—can be decent and honorable.

CHAPTER 40 | SWEEP IT AWAY

I hate housework, especially vacuuming. I just spent the day cleaning my house. I used to have a cleaning service when I had a job where I went someplace else to work. Back then, every two weeks I would run around the house frantically picking up piles of papers, dirty clothes, and disarray so the service could come in and clean. At least it was a schedule.

Now that I'm an independent contractor, I have my office in my home. I no longer have a cleaning service, so I pay very little attention to the piles that keep piling up. But sooner or later, my attention is drawn to the decorative spills on the kitchen floor or the delicate layer of dust covering the coffee table, and I realize that it's time to…have company! So I make a phone call and invite friends to come visit us. That's the impetus I need to clean my house; otherwise, it would never get done. I can easily ignore the spills on the kitchen floor, but I certainly don't want anyone else to see them.

My mother used to have a cross-stitch saying on the family room wall: *A perfectly kept house is evidence of a misspent life.* I wholeheartedly agree with that one. But there are times when sweeping the floors, dusting the furniture, clearing away the clutter— or anything physical— is just what I need to put my mental attitude back in harmony. If my thoughts are jumbled or confused, my mood reflects the discord. The physical process of putting part of my house in order also has the wonderful effect of putting my thoughts in order and lifting my mood.

I'll bet it would work for you, too. The next time you are in a sour mood because of muddled thoughts, tackle the house, yard, or garden for a little while instead of thinking. It just might clear your head and lift your mood, too. And, as an added bonus, a portion of your living environment will be clean and in order. That, in itself, is a good feeling.

CHAPTER 41 | STILL GET A THRILL

*O*n February 14, 1989, my husband Grundy came home from work with a heart-shaped box of premium chocolates, a dozen red roses in a long white box tied with a ribbon, and a beautifully wrapped present in signature pink and white stripes—lingerie! All three on the same day, for the same occasion. I was in shock.

After the initial delight and surprise, I started asking questions to explain this unusual treatment. No, he hadn't purchased a new gun, power tool, or golf club. No, he hadn't forgotten to make the house payment. No, he hadn't wrecked my car. This was just out of character for him. He is not a gift giver. But it was so romantic, and I was thrilled.

The next weekend we had dinner with two other couples who were close friends. The ladies were talking and discovered that all three of us had received identical Valentine presents—the same box of candy, dozen roses, and lingerie in the *same* color! We confronted our husbands and found out they were planning a fishing trip for the spring! And it had been Jerry's idea to go all out for the Valentine's Day extravaganza to ensure our approval of the trip. Jerry (the only romantic one) even bought all three sets of gifts and delivered them wrapped and ready for giving to the other two men. All they had to do was sign the card and write him a check. Can you imagine being the salesclerk at the lingerie store helping a man who purchased three identical gifts then asked that they be individually wrapped? I bet she thought he was a real Casanova!

Needless to say, I've never had a Valentine surprise quite like that one again. But I still get a thrill just thinking about my husband walking through the door with all those romantic gifts. (And yes, they went on the fishing trip with our blessings.)

Thrill is the exhilarating sensation you feel in moments of high enjoyment. You could be thrilled by a tender relationship connection, a physical adventure, a work or personal triumph, a travel experience, or receiving unexpected presents. Thrills build powerful memories that enrich your soul. You can replenish your emotional state by remembering past experiences and the reminiscence will still give you a thrill. Dip into your memory bank.

- Picture the face of someone you love. Remember a blissful connection. See that person smiling at you. Feel them loving and accepting you.

- Visualize a euphoric vacation spot—the beach, mountains, or lake. In your mind, see all the beautiful details of this relaxing and re-energizing place.

- Think of the "Our Song" of you and your mate. Play the music and lyrics in your head. Relive the moment you first heard the song and re-experience those "on cloud nine" feelings.

- Recall a joke, humorous incident, or a funny experience. Laugh and enjoy it again. Isn't it funny how funny things get funnier the more you recall them with family or friends? Besides feeling good, laughter works out all your major internal systems, oxygenates your blood, and relaxes your muscles.

- Bring to mind a peak physical or mental performance when you (or a loved one since you can vicariously experience the victories of others) surpassed your personal best.

- Remember when someone surprised you with an unexpected visit, assistance, or gifts. Or recall your own delight when you surprised someone.

- Evoke the feeling of holiness and wholeness you have experienced in prayer, meditation or connection to the Universal Source.

Always be ready for new thrills. Create the occasions for enjoyment. Plan get-togethers, physical adventures, or cultural experiences with family and friends. Take on a work or community challenge that is meaningful to you. Make plans for travel to exciting, beautiful, or holy places. Face new opportunities for enjoyment with an open heart and mind. Sometimes the best laid plans don't work out as you expect. Drop the expectations, continue to plan for exciting experiences and be thankful when enjoyment and thrills come your way.

Thrills, and memories of thrills, bring a burst of positive emotion. An influx of happy feelings can make you smile. A smile is the absolute best thing for your appearance. A smile opens your jaw and relaxes your face. It makes you look better and improves your body language. Most importantly, a genuine smile creates a positive opinion about you in the minds of others.

In times when your inner peace is challenged by disruptions, the inappropriate behavior of others or distressing situations, recall a happy moment. You can still get a thrill and your integrity will be restored.

CHAPTER 42 | REACH NEW HEIGHTS

"In looking for people to hire, you look for three qualities: integrity, intelligence, and energy. And if they don't have the first, the other two will kill you."

-Warren Buffet

Integrity is the virtue that helps you integrate your behavior with your beliefs and values. It is the state of being whole—when your thoughts, actions, feelings, moods, and attitudes are integrated and positive. Delve into your inner place of safety and define your personal goals for integrity. Do you support the role of emotional stability in creating a safe environment? Are you taking charge of your mood and attitude? Do you understand and practice ways to handle negative feelings and invite positive feelings? Would you be a happier and more productive person if you were in a positive emotional state more often? Quit making the same emotional mistakes over and over again. Take responsibility for the way you feel. Take the right risks to understand your feelings and correct your errors.

If you are stuck in negative feelings, your behavior can be less than honorable. Don't live your life feeling bad. If it is difficult for you to let go of long-standing negative feelings, you may need professional help (psychotherapy, counseling, touch therapy, or body work) to feel better. It's also helpful to attend seminars, read books or listen to CDs on personal growth topics. If you need to, seek assistance to heal your feelings. Your mood should not be dependent upon junk food, alcohol, or shopping. In the words of the Persian poet Rumi: *The mood you are looking for is inside of you.*

You are in charge of your mental state. Know how to keep it affirmative and hopeful.

Get back in the swing of integrity with a few pushes to get you pumping and gliding on your own. Get emotionally fit. The following is a quick reminder of the nine strategies in this section:

- **Get Down to the "Real Nitty Gritty":** Make integrity the basis for your behavior.

- **Recognize the Signals:** Remember that negative emotions are signals to help you protect yourself and correct errors.

- **Keep Your Cool:** Keep your integrity intact by defusing stress when it happens.

- **Cop an Attitude:** Understand that attitude is produced by your thoughts.

- **Restructure Your Mental Interrogation:** Learn how to pose better questions in your mind.

- **Make Grief as Brief as Possible:** Let go of the grief of losing and hold on to the happiness of loving.

- **Fire Your Trespassers:** Kick out guilt and forgive yourself and others.

- **Learn to Affirm:** Use simple statements to affirm your abilities.

- **Sweep It Away:** Use the physical process of cleaning to sweep negative thoughts and feelings away.

- **Still Get a Thrill:** Remember your moments of enjoyment and create opportunities for new thrills.

Take control of your emotional state and handle life's challenges with grace and **INTEGRITY**. Incorporating these habits into your emotional performance can help you reach new heights......Risk it!

inspiration
Get Inspired

CHAPTER 43 | PURPOSEFUL RISKS

You've probably played with a jack-in-the-box. If the box is closed, you crank the handle to hear the tune: "All around the mulberry bush...POP goes the weasel." The clown figure pops out of the box and bobs up and down grinning at you. Then you stuff it back into the box. In the box, there is confinement by boundaries. Out of the box, there is freedom. The jack-in-the-box makes a useful analogy for the dilemma of risk. Peter Drucker defines the dilemma this way: *There's the risk you can't afford to take and there's the risk you can't afford not to take.*

Human beings need clear perimeters and high standards for health, safety, and ethical behavior. Recognized authorities (medical experts, the law, church leaders) help set and enforce necessary boundaries. Unfortunately, some people choose to challenge authority by blowing right past the boundaries. They break the law, infringe on the rights of others, abuse their own health, or shun our moral codes and behave unethically. These are the risks you can't afford to take. On this hand, honor the boundaries.

But on the other hand, get out of the box. There are no boundaries for developing your potential. There are no barriers to higher performance. You have the freedom to get learning, get along with others, get healthy, and get emotionally fit. Explore your freedom. Honor your boundaries. These are the risks you can't afford **not** to take.

Be inspired to take these risks on purpose. You will be investing in your aptitudes for higher performance: innovation, influence, immediacy, and integrity. Be willing to stretch yourself to meet the challenge even though you risk personal failure and disappointment. There is no quick fix. And there is certainly no passive role. Develop a firm, grit-your-teeth type of resolve to improve your performance. It's a pay now or pay later situation. To pay now means to pursue purposeful risk taking. If not, you will be paying later with regrets about lost opportunities, poor relationships, health problems, and remorse about what you didn't learn or do.

Look to those who truly made a difference in the world like Abe Lincoln, Susan B. Anthony, Mahatma Gandhi, Martin Luther King Jr., or Mother Teresa. They were born like you and me with the potential for great performance. The actualization of their greatness depended upon the risks they were willing to take. They said yes to opportunity, change and risk, where others would have been afraid and said no. Pearl Buck reveals: *Our real weakness is not to acknowledge the extent of our power.*

"Great achievement involves great risk."

-Dalai Lama

Power lies in the fact that you can take the right risks to improve your own life and to create healing solutions for other people.

CHAPTER 44 | CALCULATE AND FOLLOW THROUGH

*N*ot long ago, I watched a documentary about movie stunt people. It was a fascinating look at the preparations and calculations necessary to stage those fantastic action scenes in movies, like falls from tall buildings, daring rescues from burning buildings, and fights on tops of moving trains—all those things that make us say, "Wow! How did they do that?"

A good portion of the astronomical cost of action-packed movies can be attributed to the time it takes to create and design a safe plan of action for the awesome high-powered feat. Safety specialists must estimate all of the possible variables, plan for the complete safety of the participants, practice over and over again with safety devices, and finally capture the daring scene on tape. What takes our breath away and looks so gutsy, dauntless, and absolutely fearless in the movie is actually the product of much planning and calculation.

If taking action on an important goal seems dangerous or risky to you, it would be wise to follow what the experts do: calculate the risk before taking the action. Whether it means making a big financial investment, ending a relationship, or bungee jumping, the place to start is by asking the following pertinent questions:

WHY	...is this good for me?
	...is this scary?
	...should I take this risk now?
	...should I wait?
WHO	...could benefit besides me?
	...could get hurt besides me?
	...could get in trouble?
	...could mentor, coach or help me with this?
WHAT	...resources are needed?
	...options are available to me?
	...will I learn from this?
	...do I have to lose if I don't take this action?
WHERE	...should I begin?
	...are the dangers or consequences?
	...could I practice or rehearse this?
	...is the best place to learn needed skills?
WHEN	...will I receive the benefits or rewards?
	...should I get coaching or mentoring?
	...is the best time?
	...should I begin?
HOW	...can I ensure reasonable success?
	...can I deal with possible failure?
	...can I improve the plan?
	...can I develop courage and initiative?

Seizing an opportunity can be speculative and risky. Searching your brain and heart for the answers to questions like these will help you develop a more complete picture of how you perceive the opportunity and how you feel about taking a chance. You will understand what you have to gain and what you have to lose. If you believe it is in your best interests to take the risk, formulate a plan of action to meet your goal. Your plan might include getting a mentor, rehearsing, assessing your progress, developing a contingency, and, of course, keeping your sense of humor and being humble.

> *"If you want to do this thing, you have to astound yourself with personal courage every day."*
>
> *-Sir Laurence Olivier*

Planning and practicing will build your endurance— the physical and mental stamina required to withstand stress, failure, and fatigue. And it will fuel your inspiration—the courage and energy needed for creative action.

I remember taking tennis lessons and the instructor constantly saying to me: *Follow through! To get a good shot, you must follow through.* Plan your work and then work your plan. Hockey star Wayne Gretsky is famous for telling us that you *miss* 100% of the shots you don't take! Follow through. Go the distance and reap the benefits of meeting your personal goals. Have faith and optimism in your ability to constructively change yourself and your circumstances through calculation and then follow through.

CHAPTER 45 | REFLECT ON IT

*B*y reading this book, you have explored the exciting competencies that accelerate your performance. Take time for personal reflection. Give careful consideration to each of the following questions:

1. In the past week what did you achieve or do that made you feel smart, in control, and on top of things?

_____

_____

_____

_____

2. In the past week, what did you do that made you feel wonderfully creative?

_____

_____

_____

_____

3. In the past week, what happened that made you feel connected to another person?

_____

_____

_____

_____

4. In the past week, what took place in a relationship interaction where you gave another person one of your resources?

_____

_____

_____

5. In the past week, what did you do to relax and enjoy life?

_____

_____

_____

6. In the past week, what occurred that made you smile or laugh out loud?

_____

_____

_____

7. In the past week, what did you experience that made you still get a thrill?

_____

_____

_____

8. In the past week, what did you notice that had nothing to do with you?

_____

_____

_____

_____

Your responses are indicators of your **Innovation, Influence, Immediacy,** and **Integrity.** The good news is that you were performing in most of these competencies within the past week. The sad news is you might have been absent to it at the time.

It happened, but you weren't aware. You weren't paying attention. It took focused effort to direct your mind to remember what risks were presented to you and how you performed.

In *Jonathan Livingston Seagull*, the seagull named Jonathan, who has transcended the limits of being an ordinary seagull, is teaching other gulls with desire to really fly. He tells his learners: *Well, this kind of flying has always been here to be learned by anybody who wanted to discover it.*

And Jonathan ponders: *Why is it that the hardest thing in the world is to convince a bird that he is free, and that he can prove it for himself if he'd just spend a little time practicing?*

You, too, are free to take some chances on yourself. Practice the strategies. Prove it to yourself.

CHAPTER 46 | BE WILD!

*H*ave you ever, at any time in your life, been referred to as a wild child?

Wild is such a great word. I went to *The Reader's Digest Great Encyclopedic Dictionary* for a worthy definition. I found thirteen choices. I had to go past *primitive and uncivilized*, past *boisterous and unruly*, to definition #10: *Wild: Eager and excited by reason of joy and desire.* That's the perfect inspiration! Be wild.....

- *Eager* to perform and make a difference.

- *Excited* by the risks and challenges you face.

- Find *joy* in your efforts.

- Have *desire* for success.

Viewing personal challenge from this perspective will dramatically improve your odds for achievement.

My all-time, favorite song is *Born to Be Wild* performed by Steppenwolf. Because it hit the charts in the late 1960s, some people dub it as part of the drug-scene, counter-culture movement. But this song keeps showing up in movies, commercials, on the radio, and in clubs. Everyone knows this song. It speaks to the heart of risk taking.

The first stanza says: *Get your motor running. Head out on the highway. Looking for adventure in whatever comes our way.* (You were singing it, weren't you?)   Look at the lyrics closely.

1) *Get your motor running.* How many times have you looked to someone else—boss, coach, spouse, parent, or friend— to motivate you? Who is the only person who can motivate you to do anything? *You!* Here's the directive. Get your motor running. You turn it on and rev it up.

2) *Head out on the highway.* In many contexts, life is referred to as the highway, road, or path. The joy is in the journey, not the destination.   Participate in life.

3) *Looking for adventure.* The big A word, Adventure. How do you define adventure? Is it pleasure, joy, bliss, challenge, variety, exhilaration, ecstasy, contentment, enjoyment, or fun?   How much of your brain is in favor of that? No matter what your age, don't you still want to have about as much adventure in life as you possibly can?   Don't sit at home on the couch, seek it out.

> "Success is loving life and daring to live it."
> -Maya Angelou

4) *In whatever comes our way.* This is the best counsel. It shows the need to be flexible, resilient, and change-ready. You are born to be wild. Let that feeling inspire your efforts for higher performance.

CHAPTER 47 | KEEP IT ALIVE

*R*isk is an equitable concept. Gender, race, age, or culture makes no difference since everyone is a risk taker. Let me tell you about Toni. When she was 74, a couple of her 14 grandkids (Robby and Ryan, the 11-year-old twin boys) had raved about a challenging zip line swing they had discovered at a park overlooking the river. One day my husband and I were driving Toni home after a meeting and we crossed that river.

"Could we stop at this park?" she suddenly asked. "I'd like to see the zip line swing on the playground that the twins told me about."

We had some extra time, so we pulled into the park. It was almost dusk and nobody was around. We sat in the car admiring at the zip line swing. On one side was a large A-frame structure with a ladder to a platform that was about 15 feet above the ground. A heavy cord was fastened to the peak of the structure and extended to a smaller A-frame on the other side, spanning a space of a good thirty yards. There was a pulley on the cord with an attached swing. To experience the challenge, you would climb up to the platform, sit in the swing, push off and zip across the thirty yards for a thrilling ride. Old tires covering the smaller A-frame would cushion your landing. Pretty cool!

After taking in the sight, Toni tapped me on the shoulder, looked me right in the eye and said: "I'm going to try it!" She jumped out of the car and headed for the swing.

My husband panicked. "Oh my gosh, she's an old lady, she won't be able to do it. She might get hurt. What should we do?"

"Nothing." I said. "It's okay."

I had seen the look on her face. I had seen that 11-year-old gleam of adventure in her eyes—not fear or uncertainty—just pure glee. She wanted the thrill! After all she was a healthy and fit 74-year-old grandmother, still loved physical challenge, and wanted to brag to her grandkids that she had experienced the zip-line swing too. And she did it with a big smile on her face and silver hair flying. In fact, she did it three times!

Yes, I knew she'd be just fine. I had seen *that look* before. Toni is my mother. I've seen her handle risk and challenge with courage for many years. Her adventurous spirit has guided our family. She's a great role model for purposeful risk taking. And now at 83, she's still zipping!

As Duke Ellington sang: *It don't mean a thing, if it ain't got that swing.* Enjoy being in the swing of life. Use the strategies in this book to find your rhythm and expand your range of motion. Take the right risks for the right reasons. Get learning. Get along with others. Get healthy. Get emotionally fit. Purposeful risk taking will accelerate your performance, enhance your satisfaction, and boost your reputation.

I challenge you to get inspired. Keep alive your 11-year-old gleam of adventure! Experience the *zip* of taking some chances. Get up, get out, and get on with it!

Remember that nobody knows how much you have to offer—not even you—unless you find your **INSPIRATION**...Risk it!